CELTIC PARABLES

ROBERT VAN DE WEYER

CELTIC PARABLES

STORIES, POEMS & PRAYERS

Northstone

Editor: Michael Schwartzentruber
Cover design: Margaret Kyle
Interior design: Julie Bachewich
Consulting art director: Robert MacDonald

Celtic Parables: Stories, Poems and Prayers was originally published in 1997 by SPCK,
London, England.

Northstone Publishing acknowledges the financial support of the Government of
Canada through the Book Publishing Industry Development Program for its
publishing activities.

Northstone Publishing is an imprint of Wood Lake Books Inc., an employee-owned
company, and is committed to caring for the environment and all creation.
Northstone recycles, reuses, and composts, and encourages readers to do the same.
Resources are printed on recycled paper and more environmentally friendly
groundwood papers (newsprint), whenever possible. The trees used are replaced
through donations to the Scoutrees for Canada program. Ten percent of all profit is
donated to charitable organizations.

Canadian Cataloguing in Publication Data
Main entry under title:
Celtic Parables

Translated from Celtic
Includes bibliographical references.
ISBN 1–896836–25–9

1. Celtic Literature–Translations into English. 2. Christian literature, Celtic–Ireland–
Translations into English. Folk literature, Celtic–Translations into English.
I. Van de Weyer, Robert.

PB1421.C44 1998   891.6'208'03823   C98–910631–4

Published by Northstone Publishing,
an imprint of Wood Lake Books Inc.
Kelowna, BC

Printing 10 9 8 7 6 5 4 3 2 1

Printed in Canada by
Transcontinental Printing

TABLE OF CONTENTS

FOREWORD
WELCOME HOME

I remember how I felt when I first consciously encountered Celtic spirituality. I was reading a review, just a short one, of Esther de Waal's book on the Celtic tradition, *Every Earthly Blessing*, and I started to tremble. I felt like someone who has been away from home so long she has forgotten what it looks like, and then some stranger hands her a photo, blurred but recognizable. Home.

That's what Celtic spirituality is to me. Robert Van de Weyer's generous collection of Celtic parables speaks to my heart not because my maternal grandparents' surnames were MacQueen and Duncan – although I remember the yearning in my grandmother's voice when she talked about "the old country." These parables are letters from home because I am Canadian.

And I've been looking all my life for a spirituality articulating that fact.

I live in a land of trees and water, land beloved by the original people here, who understood that it was sacred. I yearned as well to say it was so. But between that statement and myself stood my own people, who made factories that dumped their waste into the rivers and who thought to "manage" forests. But the ancient Celts, my ancestors, loved Creation, loved their oak groves and the sea, knew that nature was alive and holy, filled with God, unmanageable.

When I discovered that, I knew the gap between Native spirituality and my own could be crossed. Even though my people have lived here less than a hundred years, I could belong to the land too. No wonder I trembled, coming home.

That's one reason why this island spirituality has crossed the ocean to North America with such ease. The words in these parables speak to us as North Americans. Even if we live in the city, most

of us are only a generation away from the farm,
the trap line, the fishing boat, and poetry like this
assaults us with its truth:

I walk through a meadow in June
Wild flowers stroke my legs,
Red and yellow petals caress me,
The dew on the grass washes me.

The poem's questions speak to our loneliness:

Is each tiny flower an angel?
Is each petal an angelic finger?
Are the angels cleansing me of sin?
Are the angels my lovers and friends?

And – for moderns who have mostly given up a
faraway heaven but ache increasingly for God –
the poem tells us what we dimly knew:

Here and now God is present
Here and now heaven is on earth;
Here and now eternity is present;
Here and now joy is infinite.

There's more about Celtic spirituality that makes
this collection sing for our starved North
American hearts. There's the Celtic longing for
wholeness. "Could not every village become a
small city," asks one poem, "And every city be
sprinkled with green fields?" Nor is it simply
physical, this vision of opposites held together.
Part of Celtic wisdom is the understanding that
virtue and sin, youth and age, wisdom and folly,
peace and conflict, pleasure and pain – Van de
Weyer uses them as chapter headings in this book
– are inextricably linked. This is a sighting of home
for a postmodern people sick of categories,
separations, specialities, pills. As another poem,
after some rumination, concludes gently, "Good
health involves both body and soul."

It's not that we can simply lift the wisdom from that time and place. We bring North American culture and our hungry modern idiosyncrasies to Celtic spirituality, after all; surely we see what is there differently than the seventh-century herdspeople and farmers who passed these parables on to their children. But we are still fed by them. That's proof both of Celtic spirituality's universality and the durability at its core – even refracted through 20th-century lenses.

A section on youth and age, for example, with its quirky treatise on "Reason growing dim," aims straight at our youth-addicted culture as if these parables had been written for it. And – in a culture enamored of "optics" – phrases like "the stones of my house are my witnesses...these stones are the eyes of God," remind us that God sees us our most private selves, no matter what images we present to colleagues or friends.

Robert Van de Weyer has gathered, in short, a wonderful collection of the wisdom of the Celts in narrative and poetic form. And you don't have to be a Celt to hear these parables saying, "Welcome home."

Donna Sinclair
author, *A Woman's Book of Days*

INTRODUCTION

"A pious race is the Gaelic race. The Irish Gael is pious by nature [and] sees the hand of God in every place, in every time, and in every thing." With those words Douglas Hyde introduced his remarkable collection of poems, aphorisms and stories, published almost a century ago. The Irish remain the most pious nation of Europe, if piety is judged by church attendance. And seeing God in all places, times, things and people, defines precisely that form of piety which we now call "Celtic."

Douglas Hyde was one of a number of men and women who traveled round the remote regions of Ireland in the 19th century, listening to and writing down the spiritual wisdom that had been passed from one generation to another. Others engaged in the same endeavor included Thomas Crofton Croker, the pioneer; Samuel Lover; and William Carleton; and, somewhat later, Lady Gregory; J. M. Synge; and W. B. Yeats. It was a poignant period in Irish cultural history: the ancient native tongue systematically suppressed by the British authorities, so that an oral tradition that went back into the mists of pre-history was threatened with extinction. So these redoubtable collections had a sense of urgency, striving to preserve this tradition in print before it was lost for ever.

Most of these collections enjoyed little popular success at the time of publication. And by an ironic twist some are now themselves threatened with extinction. The paper on which Douglas Hyde's book was printed has now turned brittle, and is liable to crumble as the pages are turned; so the few surviving copies are rapidly disintegrating. But happily in the late 20th century there is an explosion of interest in all things Celtic. So just as the spoken word was once passed by one generation to the next, there is now an opportunity to pass its printed equivalent from one century to the next.

I have a personal interest in this Celtic revival. Despite my foreign surname, three of my four grandparents were Irish, belonging to the decadent Anglo-Irish aristocracy from which Lady Gregory emerged. And as a boy I used to stay in their damp, decaying mansions. Even in the 1950s they still employed armies of servants, drawn from the same kind of families which Douglas Hyde, Lady Gregory and the rest visited when making their collections. As far as I can recall, the tradition of reciting poems to children had indeed died out with the Irish language. But these servants still possessed a fund of stories, mostly with a strong religious flavor, which captured my young imagination. I have remembered many of these stories, and have enjoyed passing them on to my children.

The original collectors saw themselves primarily as cultural historians. The current renewal of interest in Celtic ideas has a rather different motive. The conventional religiosity of

Western Christianity is widely felt to have become quite sterile and narrow. Thus both Christians and non-Christians alike have become hungry for fresh spiritual inspiration; and many have found nourishment in the Celtic tradition. With an earlier book, *Celtic Fire*, I sought to feed this hunger by bringing together the major texts of Celtic Christianity. The surprising success of that book prompts me to bring out a sequel.

This present book is both wider and narrower in its scope than my earlier work. It is wider in that I have plundered all the collections which I can find, plus my own childish particular – and much favored – Celtic genre: that of the parable. The passages in the gospels which are termed "parables" are earthly images, used to convey spiritual images. These take the form of stories, such as the Good Samaritan; dialogues, such as the parable of the Talent; and sustained metaphors, like that of the Sower. These are undoubtedly the most striking and popular parts of the Christian message: even those who reject or are ignorant of Christian doctrine can remember and understand Christ's parables. The ancient Celts shared this aspect of Christ's genius; so the book contains aphorisms and conversations which can be funny or disturbing, happy or sad – but always powerful and memorable.

There is a great deal of overlap between the collections: broadly the same parables may appear in several versions, each significantly different. And the stories which I heard as a boy mostly figure in one or more collections. Rather than printing parallel versions, which would be dull and irritating for the general reader, I have conflated the different versions into one. And sometimes I have taken even greater liberties, either stitching two or three parables together, or dividing one parable into two or three separate parts. This process seems to me quite consistent with the way these parables have been handed down from the past. It is also consistent with the remarkable facility which parables possess for floating around the world. As a lover of parables from wherever they come, I have found stories, similar to those told in Ireland, in Hindu, Muslim, Jewish and Buddhist collections. Parables are a kind of universal spiritual language. And, since they saw God in all places, times, things and people, the ancient Celts would rejoice at this unity.

Robert Van de Weyer

ONE

TRUTH
AND FALSEHOOD

CAUSE OF DISTRESS

Your body is as tense as a cat's,
As it stalks its prey.
Your thoughts swirl like willow branches,
Caught in the autumn winds.
Your soul is as heavy as peat,
Freshly dug from the bog.
Your heart is as dark as soil,
Sodden with the winter rains.

First understand the cause of your distress.
Only then can you be healed.

GOOD NEWS

Fame may outlast a person's life;
A person's good work may be remembered
Long after their body has rotted.

Verses from a poet's pen
May outlast the name of the poet,
As the poems are sung and repeated.
Lasting longer than fame or verses

Is the book that speaks with undying tongue.
Good news of Christ lasts for ever.

PREACHING AND CHEATING

Those who have a gift for preaching,
Often use that gift for cheating.

Proclaiming the gospel so all can understand
Is a task requiring the most precise talent.

Yet the ability to express the truth clearly
Is also the ability to express falsehood convincingly.

So beware the person who preaches on Sunday
Lest they cheat you on Monday.

MARTHA BEING MARY

We need people who search for the truth,
And we need people to proclaim it.
We need people who quietly contemplate
    God's love,
And we need people to express it.
We need people who devote their lives to prayer,
And we need people to enact those prayers.
We need people who are free from all worldly ties,
And we need people to manage our affairs.

We need both Mary and Martha.
At times every Martha must become Mary,
And every Mary must become Martha.

TELLING LIES

Sometimes we tell lies to protect the hearer:
We do not want to convey hurtful truth.
Sometimes we tell lies to protect ourselves:
We do not want others to know our truth.
In distinguishing between the two, we often lie
    to ourselves:
We pretend we are protecting others, when we
    are protecting ourselves.

If we truly love someone, no lies are right.
True love demands the truth.
When feelings are hurt, love can heal.
When lies are told, love is destroyed.

SELF-KNOWLEDGE

Repentance requires honesty:
Honesty with oneself to acknowledge one's sins
Honesty with God to confess one's sins.

Yet the commonest sin is lying:
Lying to oneself, ignoring one's sins,
Lying to others, for selfish ends.

If I am lying to myself
May God open my inward eyes to see,
And may I repent of every sin.

SELF-DECEPTION

To others I am always honest;
Myself I sometimes deceive.
To others I say what I believe to be true;
Myself I can make believe a lie.
To others my smile is intended to be sincere;
Myself I can fool into hiding my anger.
To others I always wish to do good;
Myself I can blind to my evil motives.

To be truthful, honest and sincere,
Myself I must first know.

GRASPING WATER

You cannot grasp water in your hand.
It drops through your fingers.

You cannot grasp truth in your mind.
It drops through your thoughts.

You can only possess water by drinking it,
Taking it into your body.

You can only possess truth by living it,
Taking it into your heart.

SIGNPOSTS

How do we know that Scripture is right?
How can we believe the words on its pages?
How do we know that the Gospel of Luke is true,
While the rejected Gospel of Thomas is false?

Belief cannot begin with texts on paper;
Scripture is not the foundation of faith.
Belief comes as truth is discovered;
And Scripture is a signpost on the way.

THE MAN OF THE MOUNTAIN

An old man lived near the top of a high mountain. His parents had died long ago, and since then he had lived on his own. He ate the berries and the roots that grew on the mountain, and he drank from its pure springs. One day the priest climbed up the mountain to see him.

"Old man," the priest said, "in all the years I have been here, you have never attended church. Next Sunday look down onto the village. When you see people leaving their homes and walking to church, follow them."

"All right," said the old man, "I will do as you say."

The old man often looked down from his mountain top onto the village, and prayed for the people. So the next Sunday, when he saw them going to church, he walked down the mountain and followed them. Everyone in the village had heard of the old man, but this was the first time they had ever seen him. So throughout the service everyone was staring at him.

After the service was over, people started talking to him. They could see that his heart, like the mountain water, was completely pure; no evil thought or feeling had ever entered him. He told them that he prayed for them daily; and they realized that the prosperity and harmony which their village enjoyed was due to his prayers.

"Please, old man," they said eventually, "do not come to church again. We come because we are sinners, and want to be forgiven. But you have no sin. And we are afraid that if you come regularly, our sinful ideas would infect you. We just want you to pray for us."

So the old man climbed back up the mountain, and never again attended church. He continued to pray and the village continued to prosper. The old man eventually died, but in heaven he must be continuing to pray for that village – because the village remains famous for its prosperity and harmony.

THE STONE OF TRUTH

After Patrick had visited the village of Cong to preach the gospel, he went out of the village to pray. He knelt down beside a large boulder; and after he had finished praying, he went to sleep, using the boulder as a pillow. The boulder became known as the Stone of Truth, and people never dared to tell lies if their hands or head were placed on the stone.

Many years later a man called Kerwin lived in Cong. He did not believe in God; and he despised all talk of love, peace and honesty. In his view every person should gain whatever wealth they could, and enjoy it. He lived faithfully by his own creed, stealing and cheating at every opportunity.

One night he was returning to Cong after visiting another village, where he had stolen a bag of gold. There was no moonlight, and he tripped on the Stone of Truth. The bag of gold flew out of his hand, and his head came crashing down on the stone. There was a huge gash from one side of his forehead to the other. He ran home, cursing and swearing that he had lost the gold. He put a bandage on the wound. But in the following weeks and months it never fully healed; it left a scar – a long line across his forehead.

A year later the same thing happened. But this time the wound ran from the crown of his head down to the top of his nose. And it too did not heal; so he now had a cross on his forehead. The people in the village began to mock him.

"The man who doesn't believe in God has the cross of Christ on his head," they jeered.

Kerwin hated this mockery, and he hated the Stone of Truth that had made this cross. He decided to bury the stone, digging a deep hole beside it; but the stone was too heavy for him to push into the hole. Then he covered the stone with earth. But the sheep grazing nearby scraped the earth off with their feet. In utter despair he sat down on the stone and wept.

"O God," he wailed, "what can I do? I'm in utter misery." At that moment a beggar dressed in rags passed by.

"Why are you crying out to God?" this beggar asked. "Perhaps I can help."

"Go away, you wretch," Kerwin shouted.

But the beggar refused to go. He sat down a short distance away, and took out a large crust of bread. He broke the bread into two, and handed one half to Kerwin. Without thinking what he was doing, Kerwin took the bread, and they both started to munch.

"Well," said the beggar, after they had finished eating, "you've called out to God for help, and you've taken bread from a beggar. So you can't be proud. You must be a true Christian."

At that the beggar went on his way. Only then did Kerwin realize what had happened. From that moment onwards he gave up stealing and cheating, and devoted himself to serving the needs of others. He lived to a great age. Most of the people who knew him in his evil days died; and the young people saw the cross on his forehead as a sign of his saintliness.

Shortly before he died he invited some young people into his hut, and he told them the story of how he became a Christian.

"That stone which I stumbled on," he concluded, "saved me. And that beggar gave me my first communion."

THE FISHING TEST

A farmer had a son called Kevin who was no good at farming. If Kevin tried to milk a cow, he pinched the teats so hard that the cow jumped in the air. If he tried to shear a sheep, he took off the ears and tail as well. The farmer decided that his son was too intelligent for farming; and instead he should train as a priest.

So the farmer took his son to the city, and presented him to the bishop. The bishop took Kevin to one side, and asked him a series of questions to test his religious knowledge.

"Who created heaven?" the bishop asked.

"The one who created earth," Kevin replied.

"And who created earth?"

"The one who created men and women."

"And who created men and women?"

"The one who created space for their souls in heaven."

"And who created space for their souls in heaven?"

"The one who created heaven, of course."

The bishop hit Kevin round the head, calling him an impudent fool, and sent him home. His father was even more angry than the bishop.

"You are as stupid at religion as you are at farming," the father shouted. "You're a disgrace to our family."

When they reached home Kevin was very dejected, thinking himself completely useless. In a cave a few miles away there lived a wise old hermit. Kevin decided to go and ask the hermit's advice.

"It doesn't matter what the bishop or your father think of you," the hermit said. "What matters is the truth. If God wants you to preach the gospel and comfort the sick, then this is what you must do. So we must test God's will."

The hermit took Kevin to a large lake. On the shore was a coracle, with a fishing rod inside it. The hermit instructed Kevin to go out in the coracle, and try to catch fish. Kevin did as the hermit said. For a day, a night, another day and another night Kevin sat in the coracle, holding the rod over the side. Finally a fish was caught on the hook; and Kevin pulled the fish into the boat. As soon as Kevin saw the fish with a hook in its mouth, he took pity on it. Carefully he took the hook out, and threw the fish back into the water. Then he rowed back to the shore where the hermit was waiting.

"You have proved," said the hermit, with a broad smile, "that you have the three qualities necessary to be a priest. Firstly, you are patient. If you are willing to wait two days and nights to catch a fish, you will wait two years, even two decades, to catch a soul. Secondly, you are compassionate. If you can take pity on a fish, then you will show far greater pity for humans in need. Thirdly, you are humble: even though you were the cause of the fish's distress, pride did not prevent you from saving it."

The hermit told Kevin to go back to the village and start visiting and speaking to people in

Christ's name. Since he was patient, he did not mind if some initially rebuffed him. Since he was compassionate, he was soon renowned for the help he gave to people. And since he was humble, he was content to serve people without the status of ordination by a bishop. His only concern was to help people to fill the spaces which God has created in heaven.

THE MAD PRIEST

A miller called Dennis wanted his son Owen to become a priest. So he used all the profits from the mill to send his son to college to train. After five years the son returned wearing the robes of priesthood. There was great rejoicing in the family and the whole village.

At ordination Owen had vowed to remain poor and celibate. So he was shocked to see that the priest in charge of the village owned many fields with livestock, and also had a woman living with him in his house. He learnt that the priest had bought the fields using money which poor people had contributed to the church. Owen decided that he could not work with such a wicked man. So instead of serving the people of the parish, he began to serve the animals.

At night he slept in his father's mill, which was a long way from the village. In the morning he went out into the fields to talk to the sheep and cattle. He always had with him a large Bible: he would read from this to the animals; and he put it under his head when he went to sleep.

The people at first thought he was mad. When they saw him in a field during the daytime, they laughed and jeered. After dark they were frightened to pass near the mill, for fear he might come out and attack them. But then they noticed how much the sheep and cattle loved him. The animals always gathered round, munching grass and listening to what he said.

The priest in charge of the village was so busy making money and enjoying himself that he had no time to teach the people. So two young men, hungry for true spiritual teaching, went out one day to join the animals. They were greatly inspired by what they heard, and that evening urged their friends to come out as well. Soon almost everyone in the village was going out to join the animals and listen to Owen, the mad priest. His church in the fields was packed, while the church in the village was empty.

Eventually the corrupt priest died, and the people invited Owen to replace him. So one Sunday Owen walked from the fields to the church in the village. All the sheep and cattle followed him, and entered the church with the people.

From that moment onwards the people never killed a sheep or cow for meat; they only took wool from the sheep and milk from the cows. They said that, since these animals had taught them to respect Owen's madness, they must respect the animals.

TWO

LOVE
AND HATE

SYMPHONY

There is no music so gentle,
No sound so sweet,
No praise so pleasant
Than the praise, sound and music
Of that simple word "Love."

The word itself is like a song,
It conjures images of all that is good.
On the lips it's like a soothing drink.
Let's dance, sing and play
The symphony of love.

BEING DEPENDENT

When Jesus came to earth as a baby,
He depended entirely on human love –
That of Mary, Joseph and the shepherds.

When Jesus preached and healed,
He depended entirely on human love –
The alms given by those who heard him.

I too depend on human love.
The kindness of others sustains my soul.
The gifts of others sustain my body.

Every person depends on others' love.
Let no one be ashamed of their needs.
To depend on others is to imitate Christ.

FRIENDS OF SADNESS

When I am happy, I have many friends.
I am witty in conversation, making people laugh.
I sing sweet ballads, making people cry.
So they are glad of my company.

When I am sad, I have few friends.
I become dull of mind, with nothing to say.
I become dull of heart, with no will to sing.
So people shun my company.

The friends of sadness are true friends.

KNEADING AND RISING

As I knead the flour
I think of all the many grains
That have been ground to make it.
Christ's church is like flour
Made up of many people of many races
Ground up to make a single dough.

As I watch the dough rise
I think of the yeast's power
Raising up the weight of flour and water.
Prayer in Christ is like rising dough
Drawing together every hope and fear
And lifting them up to God.

FREE KISSES

A wedding is a costly business.
Money is needed for the priest and the clerk.
Money is needed for the hire of the church.
Money is needed to feed the guests.
Money is needed for robes to wear.

Love by contrast is entirely free.
Free are the smiles that play on the lips;
Free are the kisses stolen by moonlight;
Free are the words whispered at midnight;
Free are the strolls hand in hand through the wood.

We are rich in love but poor in money.
The priests say our union is sinful.
May God, who blesses us, forgive.

MAN AND WOMAN

If God has made us all to love one another,
Is it not true that any man can love any woman,
And that any woman can love any man?

Husband, why be discontent with your wife?
Wife, why be discontent with your husband?
Whoever you are, God has made you for love.

There is no such thing as a bad marriage.
Any marriage, between any man and any woman,
Can be good if God is the master.

MARRIED TO GOD

As I lie in bed with my wife
I can sense the warmth of her body;
I can hear the steady rhythm of her breath;
I can touch her soft, smooth skin;
I can smell the sweetness of her body;
I can see the silhouette of her figure.
I love her as I love myself.

Do I love God as I love my wife?
Do I love Christ as I love myself?
Is God in Christ as near me as she?
Can I sense, hear, touch, smell and see him
As I sense, hear, touch, smell and see her?
I long to be as close to God
As I am to her – and closer still.

HELL'S PURSUIT

Hell pursues each person every day.
Even the holiest priest has hell on his tail.
Anger snaps at the heels.
Sloth is like lead on the hands.
Greed claws at the stomach.
Pride is like air in the head.
Lust throbs in the bowels.
Hatred is like brine in the lungs.
You cannot escape hell by running.
Love alone can slay it.

A MAN COMES HOME

A man comes home at dusk.
He has worked hard in the fields all day.
His children are screeching and screaming.
His wife grumbles and moans.

He sits down on his old wooden chair.
He quietly mends a hole in his breeches.
His children still screech and scream.
His wife grumbles and moans.

His wife hands him some food.
No words are said as he eats.
His children still screech and scream.
His wife grumbles and moans.

If only they could converse,
Quietly, calmly, patiently.
If only they could embrace,
Warmly, gently, lovingly.

GRANTING A WISH

A holy man arrived in the village on Christmas Eve. A bitter cold wind was blowing from the north. The holy man knocked on the door of the first cottage he saw. It belonged to Brendan and his wife, Maureen. They urged him to come in and share their Christmas dinner. So that evening the three of them sat down at the table, and ate a wonderful meal. The next morning the holy man said that he must be on his way. Brendan and Maureen begged him to stay longer. But he insisted. So Maureen gave him a large breakfast, so he would have ample energy for his journey. As he was leaving the holy man turned to Brendan and Maureen.

"Tell me the thing you most wish God to provide you in this life," he asked.

Brendan and Maureen had never before wondered what mattered to them most in life. For a few moments they stood in silence. Then Brendan spoke.

"Maureen and I often bicker about silly little things."

"Yes," added Maureen. "Our lives would be perfect if we were always loving and affectionate towards one another."

"And if we never picked silly quarrels with our neighbor," Brendan said laughing.

"Then," said the old man, "your wish shall be granted."

Sure enough, from that moment onwards Brendan and Maureen stopped arguing, and lived in peace. And their lives became happy and contented.

A year later on Christmas Eve the holy man again arrived in the village. This time he knocked on the door of Nathan and Martha. They were a mean, nasty couple. But they had heard about the holy man visiting Brendan and Maureen: how he had asked them their dearest wish, and how that wish had been granted. So they welcomed the holy man into their house, in the hope that they would benefit in the same way.

When it was time for dinner Nathan politely asked the holy man to sit at the head of the table. In the kitchen Martha cut the best pieces of meat from the joint, for herself and Nathan to eat later, and brought in the rest.

"Sir," Martha said, as she served the holy man, "we're having the best meat in the house – in honor of you."

The next morning the holy man said he must leave. Nathan and Martha did not press him to stay. They simply stood in front of him, waiting for him to ask them their dearest wish. The holy man slowly put on his cloak; and then just as he was leaving he asked them the same question which he had asked Brendan and Maureen. But no sooner had the holy man asked the question, than Nathan and Martha began to argue: she wanted silk dresses and velvet gowns, while he wanted a bigger farm and more cows.

"Why can't I have nice clothes to wear, and beautiful jewelry? – I've worked hard for you all my life," Martha screamed, stamping her feet.

"Because I want to be the biggest and most important farmer in the whole district," Nathan yelled back.

While they were shouting at each other, the holy man quietly slipped away. For another ten minutes they continued to argue, and only then did they notice he had gone. They stared at each other in silence, realizing what fools they were.

"We've spent all our lives bickering," Martha sobbed, breaking the silence.

"And look where it's got us," Nathan added.

A year later on Christmas Eve the holy man again came to the village, and again he called on Nathan and Martha. Now they were genuinely delighted to see him. And Nathan ran out to tell Brendan and Maureen that the holy man had returned, inviting them to come to dinner. Martha served the finest meat, giving her guests the best bits. And they all had a wonderful evening. As they were about to go to bed, Martha turned to the holy man. "Since you came to visit us," she said, "our lives have become so much happier. I don't know what you have done, but I want to thank you."

"Yes," the other three added, "we all want to thank you."

"I have done nothing," the holy man said with a smile. "For the first time you've said to yourselves that peace brings happiness. And when a person says this with all their heart, the wish becomes the action – and the action brings the result."

AN ACT OF GRATITUDE

A very old man went out one day onto the land beside his house, and began planting fruit trees. A young man walked by.

"What are you doing?" the young man asked.

"Planting fruit trees," the old man replied.

"But you will not see fruit in your lifetime," the young man said.

"The fruit that I have enjoyed in my lifetime," the old man answered, "has been from trees that people before me planted. So to express my gratitude of them, I am planting trees to give fruit to those who come after me."

THE KING'S LOVE

In a remote village lived a beautiful girl. Her parents were poor peasants, who could only afford to give her rags for clothes. But even in rags she looked like a princess.

One day the king rode through the village on a hunting expedition. He saw the beautiful peasant girl, and immediately fell in love with her. He jumped off his horse, and asked her to marry him. She was wise beyond her years, and knew that he would soon tire of her beauty. So at first she refused him. But he implored her.

"Very well, your majesty," she said, "come back tomorrow, and I will give you my answer."

The king rode off. Her parents insisted that she should marry the king; and she realized that for their sake she must do so, in order to have the wealth to keep them into their old age. So she began to wonder how she could turn the king's physical attraction for her into a love that would last. At dawn the next day the king returned, and fell on his knees before her.

"What is your answer?" he begged.

"I will marry you on one condition," she replied, "that if ever you should drive me away from the palace, you will let me take whatever I love most."

The king readily agreed to her condition. And a week later, with the peasant girl dressed like a true princess, they were married.

As she had predicted, the king eventually grew tired of her beauty; and his lust turned to sullen indifference. He began to pick quarrels with her; and one evening a quarrel turned into a blazing row.

"I can stand you no longer," the king roared. "You must leave the palace and return to your hovel."

"I will be back in my hovel tomorrow," she replied. "But I will make you keep your promise – to let me take whatever I love most."

The king was accustomed to drink at bedtime a herbal potion, prepared by his wife, to help him sleep. On this occasion she made it especially strong, so he slept very soundly. She asked her servants to lift the sleeping body into a carriage; and she rode in the carriage back to her parents' home.

The following morning when the king awoke he had no idea where he was.

"Where am I?" he shouted. "Have I been kidnapped?" His wife came to the bed.

"I am in my hovel," she replied, "just as you ordered. But according to your promise, I have brought with me from the palace that which I love most."

The king was filled with shame. He took her into his arms. Later that day they returned to the palace, and lived in loving harmony for the rest of their days.

THREE

VIRTUE
AND SIN

GOD'S LAWS

Where are God's laws?
Are they found in a book?
Is the gospel a book of law?

What are God's laws?
Are they a set of rules?
Is salvation blind obedience?

God's law is in our hearts.
It is our desire for goodness.
The gospel helps that desire to grow.
Salvation is its harvest.

TIME TO CHANGE

There is always time to change.
Dull dreary sin can last for years.
But goodness can come in a flash.

The angels are ready to greet you.
The Spirit is ready to come to you.
Her flames are ready to touch you.

Let those flames burn your skin.
Let the Spirit enter your soul.
Let the angels embrace you.

CONTROLLING THE HEART

The priests tell me
That if I sin with my will and inclination,
It is as if the deed is done.

My conscience tells me
That if I want to sin, yet restrain myself,
God will bless me for my virtue.

Does sin lie in the heart or in action?
Minute by minute I can control my actions.
It takes a lifetime and more to control the heart.

BECOMING TRUSTWORTHY

A person who has once committed theft is
    always distrusted.
Yet if they later learn to control their greed,
They are more trustworthy than a person who
    has never been tested.

A person who has committed adultery is
    always condemned.
Yet if they later learn to control their lust,
They are a better spouse than a person who
    has never been tempted.

It can be better to sin and be forgiven,
Than never to have sinned.

HOW HAVE YOU SPENT YOUR DAY?

How have you spent your day?

You have been working hard, but for whose sake?
You have been tilling the soil, but for what
    purpose?

There is no virtue in work; only in its aims.

Eat now, to refresh and comfort your body.
Then sit down, and reflect on your aims.
The truth may frighten you, but do not flinch.
You will rise tomorrow with fresh vigor.

I HAVE NEVER DONE ANYTHING

I have never done anything deserving much blame.
I have not lied or cheated; I have been faithful to
    my spouse.
I have given alms to the poor, and food to
    the hungry.
I have won the respect of all upright citizens.

I have never done anything deserving much praise.
I have made no sacrifices; I have always been
    comfortable.
I have used only surplus wealth to help the needy.
I have not stood up against injustice.

I envy the sinner who repents.
Can I repent my dullness?

FACT OF LIFE

I am not ashamed to be a sinner;
Sin is a fact of life.
I do not try to hide my faults;
My faults are God's creation.

So when I sin, I confess freely
To all I have hurt and wronged.
They must then forgive me,
As sinners like myself.

THE HUMAN SENSES

The blind person learns to hear more acutely;
From faint echoes they can find their way.
The deaf person learns to see more acutely;
From movement of the lips they can understand.
The person who gains little pleasure from things
    of God
Strives to take greater pleasure in material things.
The person who finds little pleasure in material
    things
Learns to take greater pleasure in things of God.
That is why those who love God
Must learn to restrain bodily desires.

BUCKLING LEGS

My legs are buckling under the weight of my sins.
Like a load of boulders strapped to my back,
I carry this burden all day and every day.
How can I loosen the straps and release myself?

I will allow my knees to bend and fall,
And let the burden press me to the ground.
If the straps stay tight, I shall be crushed and die.
If the straps loosen, I shall rise and live.

AN ACHING TOOTH

Toothache starts in a rotten tooth,
Then the pain spreads through the jaw
Until one's whole head starts to throb.
Every thought is filled with toothache.

Sin starts with a rotten action,
Then the pleasure spreads through the body
Until the soul itself becomes enslaved.
Every feeling is filled with sinful desire.

Pull out the aching tooth.
Root out the sinful action.

A SOLDIER TO HIS GENERAL

When I come to God to confess my sins,
Do I need to lie face down on the ground?
Should I grovel and abase myself before God?

God allowed sin and evil into this world;
God gave me freedom to choose good or bad;
God put selfish desires in my breast.

The challenge of sin is the purpose of life;
The war against sin gives life its zest.
Without evil I could not know goodness.

I come to God as a soldier to his general;
I ask God for stronger weapons in battle,
God inspires me to fight – my head is held high.

THE HAG AND THE LOUT

The hag   From your father I got nothing but drunken insults and shame. And you are no better.

The lout   It was your fault for going with him. And you didn't even marry him. What can an immoral woman like you expect?

The hag   I was poor. I sold my body to him – and you are the result.

The lout   You are still poor. Now you are reduced to begging by the side of the road. So what good has your prostitution done you?

The hag   I have repented my past sins. I do not expect God to reward me with riches. Poverty is my penance.

The lout   You are always the victim. Once you were the victim of poverty. Now you are God's victim – and God keeps you poor.

The hag   You are no better than me. You don't even beg. You just live off the alms which

I obtain. Why don't you get off your bottom and work? You're young enough to earn a good living.

The lout I don't need to work with you to beg for me.

The hag So why don't you turn to religion and find joy in being virtuous? There's no joy in sin.

The lout Virtue and sin, goodness and evil – what is the difference? Your life was miserable when you were a sinner. Now you're virtuous and still miserable.

The hag I look miserable because I am dressed in rags, my hair is matted and my face lined. But I have the peace of an easy conscience.

The lout An easy conscience and an empty belly!

The hag You have a troubled conscience and an empty belly.

The lout You're wrong. I have no conscience. And I've learned to numb the pangs of hunger when you give me no bread.

The hag   Then you're dead, even though you are living.

The lout   You may be living – but you might as well be dead.

The hag   You are right – death is my hope – it's what I live for.

THE BLUE SCARF

At the feast of the Annunciation, all the young virgins in the village put on a blue scarf, as a sign of their devotion to the Virgin Mary. One girl, who herself was called Mary, was in her room putting on her blue scarf, when her younger brother burst in. The boy grabbed the scarf and began to use it as a skipping rope.

"That is a holy scarf," the girl exclaimed. "Give it back to me at once."

But the boy, whose name was Michael, continued to skip over it, laughing and shouting.

"You are committing a sin," the girl went on. "You must fast all day Friday as a penance."

Eventually their mother, hearing the commotion, came in and ordered Michael to hand Mary back the scarf. And she led them off to mass. On the way, Mary, who was a pious girl, reminded her brother that he must fast on Friday.

"From dawn till dusk, no food or drink must pass your lips," she said, wagging her finger.

Two days later, on Thursday, Michael became ill with a high fever and went to bed. Mary nursed him. She decided that, despite his fever, she would compel him to fast on Friday. So she told her mother not to cook any food for Michael, as she would prepare whatever he needed. Her mother had no idea of her intentions.

From dawn on Friday, Mary took her brother no food and no drink. Without water his fever grew steadily worse. Sweat poured from his body until he was so dry he could sweat no more. But Mary remained convinced that Michael must complete the penance for his wicked act.

"If I relent now," she said to herself, "he will think he can get off lightly in the future – so he will sin again."

As the sun began to set over the western horizon, Michael's breathing grew slower and heavier. Then as the sun disappeared, his breathing stopped; he was dead. When Mary realized what had happened, she rushed and told her mother. Then she ran to the priest, and confessed to him.

Many people accused Mary of murder; and she accepted the accusation. But she was not arrested; so she had to impose her own penance on herself. From dawn until dusk every day she ate and drank nothing – except when she was ill. Never again did she pass judgment on others.

"No sin is worse than what I have committed," she would say, "so I should be judged, not judge."

And she wore a blue scarf, not just on the feast of the Annunciation, but every day, to remind herself of how, in her pride, she had betrayed the Virgin Mary.

THE HONEY POT

An old woman came to visit a priest, who was rather fat.

"I am in despair," the old woman said. "My son spends all our money on honey, which he eats straight from the pot. We are penniless. Please come and tell him to stop."

Weeks passed, and the priest did not come. The old woman thought the priest must have forgotten her request. So she went to see him again. As soon as she came through his door, she was amazed at the sight of him.

"You are so thin," she exclaimed. "What's wrong with you?"

"I have given up buying honey and eating it from the pot," the priest replied. "Now that I know I can stop, I will come and tell your son to stop as well."

HEALING WORDS

A traveling preacher visited a village where, in one of the large houses, a young girl lay seriously ill. Her parents invited the preacher to visit her. The preacher knelt at the young girl's bed, and said a prayer. Then he rose.

"Now the girl will start to recover," the priest said to the parents.

An uncle of the girl was standing nearby. He was skeptical about spiritual matters, and pinned his hopes on drugs and medicines.

"How can a few words make a sick person well?" the uncle scoffed.

To the uncle's surprise, the preacher turned to him, his eyes blazing with fury.

"You understand nothing," the preacher shouted. "You're an ignorant fool."

The uncle was deeply offended at this rudeness. His face went red, and he began to shake and sweat. Then the preacher's face broke into a smile.

"When a few words can make a man like you hot and angry," the preacher said, "why do you doubt the power of a few words to make a young girl well?"

FOUR

FAITH
AND DOUBT

I CANNOT BELIEVE

Will God condemn those who do not believe?
Will God reject those who do not conform?
Must people accept the creeds of religion?
Must they believe as the priests demand?

I cannot believe all I am taught.
I cannot live without breaking the rules.
But my soul yearns to know God.
And my heart cherishes all God has made.

Surely God will put honesty above belief.
Surely God will place love above conformity.

FRIENDSHIP WITH CHRIST

A person who approaches Christ with flattery
    makes no impression.

One who pretends to moral virtue is seen for what
    they are.
A person who takes pride in religious observance
    is not respected.

One who demands friendship is gently spurned.

Friendship with Christ cannot be claimed, but only
    received.
It is not a right, but a privilege.
Open your heart to Christ, and he will enter.
Come to him on your knees, and he will raise
    you up.

WAS THE VALLEY THERE?

Was the valley there before the river flowed;
Or did the river cut the valley?

Was the sand there before the waves roared;
Or did the waves break rocks into sand?

Did books come before people wrote;
Or did authors first create books?

Did marriage come before children were born;
Or did children cause people to marry?

Can I love my neighbors before I meet them;
Or do neighbors stir my heart?

Can I pray before I know God;
Or docs God tell me to pray?

GRAINS OF SAND

How many grains of sand on the beach?
How many blades of grass in the meadow?
How many drops of dew on the tree?
If you could count all these,
You could count the number of God's blessings.

Do not even try to count.
Just trust,
And enjoy,
And give thanks.

THE THINGS OF GOD

You may have a highly polished shoe,
But your footsteps are no grander
Than those made by a barefoot person.

You may have a fine woollen cloak,
But naked your body is no different
From that of a person dressed in rags.

God made the foot, people the shoe.
God made the body, people the cloak.
Cherish the things of God above those of people.

RIGHT BEING WRONG

Christians often argue about what they believe.
Some believe one doctrine, some another.
One group strives to convince other groups
That it alone possesses the truth.

Yet God alone possesses the truth,
Because God alone is the truth.
On earth we see only glimpses, hints;
Our knowledge of truth is partial.

So the different groups who argue
May all be right and all be wrong:
Right in seeing one part of the truth;
Wrong in claiming the whole.

PROTECTION ON A JOURNEY

When I set out on a journey,
I offer seven prayers.
I pray that God will protect me
From falling into a river and drowning,
From getting lost and dying of cold,
From being attacked and beaten by robbers,
From gambling and losing my money,
From contracting a terrible fever,
From being tempted by sexual favors,
From making friends with evil people.

I am too stupid and too weak
To protect myself.
God alone can guard me,
And bring me safely back home.

LAZY CLERGY AND FAT FRIARS

Do not foist your religion on me, you lazy clergy.
On weekdays you hunt and fish, and you
    chase girls.
Then on Sunday you dress in robes and stand
    at the altar.
Why should I come on Sunday to join your pious
    chants,
When for the rest of the week you mock the
    words you uttered?

Do not foist your religion on me, you fat friar.
Your desire for food and drink rules your daily life.
Then on Sunday you ask forgiveness and promise
    to reform.
Why should I come on Sunday to join your humble
    pleas,
When for the rest of the week you mock the
    words you uttered?

LOW, HIGH AND DEEP PRAYERS

I send low prayers along the ground.
These are for Jesus Christ;
Asking him to heal all people.

I send high prayers into the sky.
These are for our God in heaven,
Asking God to bring peace to the world.

I send deep prayers into my heart.
These are for the Holy Spirit
Asking the Spirit to heal and pacify my heart.

PRAYING WITH THE SPIRIT

Sometimes when I pray, I utter the words,
But I do not feel or think them.
Sometimes when I pray, I utter the words,
Thinking about what I say, but not feeling.
Sometimes when I pray, I utter the words,
And I both think and feel what I say.

An act of will cannot make me feel,
Nor stop my mind from wandering.
An act of will can only make me utter.
So I shall utter the words,
And let the Spirit do the rest,
Guiding my mind and heart as it wills.

IMPROVING RELIGION

We say we want to improve our religion.
We clamor for fresh ideas in our faith.
We imagine that we understand more than
    our ancestors,
And we look with pity at their ignorant mistakes.

Yet how can we improve on the teaching of Patrick?
How can we be fresher than the freshness of Brigit?
How can we have deeper understanding
    than Columba?
We should look with pity at our own mistakes.

COMPLEX DOCTRINES

I am full of doubt; yet I trust in God.
I cannot believe all I am taught.
The doctrines of the church are complex.
Some I cannot understand.
Some seem to make no sense.
Some make sense, but are implausible.

The priest may tell me I'm a sinner;
And may inform me that good people believe –
That doubt is a sign of sin.
Yet I trust in God.
God's love makes sense.
God's love is confirmed by many blessings.

DIFFERENT RELIGIONS

There are different religions in our land.
People believe their own is best.
Sometimes they tolerate other religions,
Sometimes they despise other religions,
Sometimes they fight other religions.

God speaks to us in different ways.
God chooses the best way for each person.
Let us rejoice in different religions,
Let us give thanks for different religions,
Let us love different religions.

HOME

Where is my home?
Is it the house where I live,
The garden where I sit in summer,
The country where I roam,
Or the church where I worship?

The place I call home
Is where my heart is at rest.
And my heart is most at rest
When it turns to God in prayer.
So wherever I pray is home.

PRIEST AND PEOPLE

A good priest died.
His people greatly mourned him;
And they missed his love.
"Who shall visit our sick,
And conduct our worship?"
They asked in despair.
Years passed, no one came.
Worship ceased in their church,
And the sick died unblest.

Then the people gathered.
They stopped mourning the past
And instead looked to the future.
"We will visit our sick,
And will conduct our worship,"
They said with courage.
Worship resumed in their church,
And the sick were always blest.
Years passed, and the people thrived.

TWO OLD WOMEN

Maurya   A hundred welcomes, Sheela. You look anxious. What is troubling you? What's your news?

Sheela   I have no news. It's not news that's troubling me.

Maurya   What is it then?

Sheela   It's you that's troubling me, Maurya. We're both old women now, and soon will die. But you have no fear of God.

Maurya   Why should I fear God? If God exists, God loves me. If God doesn't exist, then there's nothing to be frightened of anyway.

Sheela   How dare you speak that way! May God's ears be closed to your blasphemy. And when did you last go to mass or confession?

Maurya   Why should I go to mass? The priest is a hypocrite: he tells people to be good and holy, but he's no better than the next person. I would not confess my sins to a hypocrite.

Sheela   What will happen when you die? Will you not have a priest to help you?

Maurya   When I'm dying I don't want a priest. I want my children around me.

Sheela   Anyone would think you had no religion in you at all. Yet I know you well – and you're a good and kind woman.

Maurya   Why do you link goodness with religion? Religion doesn't make people good; often it makes people bad. Look at the way different churches and religions squabble and argue.

Sheela   Religion teaches you what is true and what is false, what is good and what is bad.

Maurya   How do you know your religion is true, and that what it teaches is good? You only belong to it because you grew up in it.

Sheela   I don't know for certain. All I know is that I need religion.

Maurya   All I know is that I need all religions or none.

THE PRIEST AND THE TINKER

Priest   You're a man in your middle years, and
          not yet baptized. I want to baptize you.

Tinker   And what good would baptism do me?
          I've been well enough without it until
          now.

Priest   It would lift the burden of sin from your
          shoulders.

Tinker   My burden is this anvil I carry from
          place to place to ply my trade. I carry no
          burden of sin.

Priest   We all carry a burden of sin. We were
          born sinners, destined for eternal
          punishment. Only baptism can save you.

Tinker   I commit no sin. I'm honest. I charge only
          a fair wage for a fair day's work. I give
          what I can to the needy.

Priest   Good behavior can't save you from hell;
          only God can save you, and take you to
          heaven.

Tinker	And who created this hell and this heaven?
Priest	God did.
Tinker	You mean God created hell in order to punish people. And he punishes good people as well as bad. This God seems very strange.
Priest	It is not for us to question the ways of God.
Tinker	I'm not clever enough to question God's ways. But from what you've told me, I want nothing to do with God.

THE STRANGE WILL

A wise old priest, who had served a particular village for many decades, knew that he would soon die. He knew that there were many stupid and boneheaded priests in the land and he was anxious lest his successor should be one of these. So he wrote a will, in which he gave instructions as to how his successor should be found.

The old priest duly died. And after the funeral, all the people gathered on the village green to hear the will. The priest had owned 17 horses, which were kept in a field behind the church; and the people were keen to hear who would now have them.

"The 17 horses," the will began, "shall be divided between three people, in the following way. The sexton shall have half, the beadle one third, and the choirmaster one ninth."

There was silence as people tried to work out what this meant. They made all sorts of calculations on their fingers and toes, and eventually reached the conclusion that 17 horses couldn't be divided in this way. Someone suggested that the horses be sold, and the money divided; but others replied that this would go against the terms of the will. After much discussion it was decided that the three men, the sexton, the beadle and the choirmaster, should go in search of someone who had sufficient wisdom and intelligence to interpret the old priest's will.

For many weeks the three men walked from village to village, putting their problem to everyone they met. No one could find the solution.

Finally they met a young man, still living with his parents, who gave the answer.

"I will give you my horse," the young man said, "and that will make 18. Then the sexton can have half, which is nine horses. The beadle can have a third, which is six horses. The choirmaster can have a ninth which is two horses. That makes 17. So there is one left over – my horse – which you can return to me."

So the three men took the young man and his horse back to their village; and they did as he suggested. The people were astonished. Then they realized why their old priest had made such a peculiar will. By this means a successor of wisdom and intelligence had been found – the young man.

The young man served as priest for many decades. Over that time he had acquired 17 horses. By the time he died, as a very old man, all the old inhabitants had already died. So he was able to make an identical will – with the same happy result.

THE DISTRACTED PRIEST

A priest was kneeling at a roadside shrine just outside the town, saying his prayers. A young woman passed very close to the shrine, and distracted the priest.

"You insolent girl," the priest shouted out. "Can't you see I'm saying my prayers? Why do you have to disturb me when I'm praying?"

"I'm very sorry, Father," the young woman said; "I didn't notice you. I'm on my way to see my young man; and I was thinking about him."

"I was thinking about God," the priest said piously.

An elderly man who was also traveling along the road heard this exchange.

"The young woman was thinking about her man," the elderly man said to the priest, "and didn't notice you. You were thinking about God, and noticed her. If you loved God with the same devotion as she loves her man, you could share this road in peace."

THE DRUNKARD

Kate was the mother of five children living in a small cottage. Her husband, Bertie, was a drunkard who spent almost every penny he earned at the tavern. So the children never had enough to eat; and they dressed in rags.

A holy man was passing through the village, and saw Kate sitting outside her cottage, quietly weeping. He sat beside her, and asked her to tell him what was wrong. She told him about her drunken husband.

The holy man went to the tavern, where Bertie had just arrived.

"Your wife Kate has just told me about you," the holy man said. "I tell you, that if you continue this drinking you shall turn into a mouse."

Bertie felt ashamed, and immediately left the tavern and began walking back home. But on his way he met an old friend, who had left the village many years previously, and had now returned to visit his family. The two men embraced.

"Now you must tell me everything you've been doing," said Bertie.

"Let me buy you a drink," the friend said, "and then I'll give you all my news."

So they walked arm in arm to the tavern. Four hours later they were both very drunk, and Bertie staggered back home. As he entered his cottage he saw their black cat on the kitchen table. He remembered what the priest had said – and a look of terror came over his face.

"Get that cat out of here," he shouted, "or it'll eat me up."

And from that moment onwards he never drank a drop.

THE ABSENT FERRY

One evening a priest was standing on the bank of the River Shannon waiting for the ferry to take him to the other side. A man came to him.

"Father," the man said, "the ferry is a long time coming. I am in a hurry to get home as my child is unwell. What should I do?"

"If I knew what to do, I wouldn't be here myself," the priest replied.

"But there must be some way I can get home," the man persisted.

"How many times have I said from the pulpit that if a person has faith they can do anything?" the priest said.

There was silence. The man felt he had irritated the priest. Still the ferry did not come. Both men began to suspect that the ferryman had stopped for the night. Then the man spoke again.

"Is it really true that a person who has faith can do anything?"

"Of course it is," the priest snapped back.

The man stepped out into the river and walked across it.

"The greatest darkness is beneath the lamp itself," the priest said to himself. And he went off to seek an inn where he could stay the night.

JUDGMENT ON FOLLY

Three merchants, called O'Flynn, O'Leary and O'Connell, had made 10,000 gold sovereigns by their dealings. They had worked hard together for ten years, and decided they should have a holiday for one year. So they divided 1,000 gold sovereigns between them, to spend on their holiday; and they took 9,000 to a goldsmith called Joseph to keep in his strongroom. Joseph agreed to look after their money for a year, and not to give it to any one of them except in the presence of the two others. The three merchants then went their separate ways.

Six months later O'Flynn came to Joseph's house late one night, and banged on the door. When Joseph answered, O'Flynn said that all the money was needed urgently, as they had the opportunity of buying valuable cargo.

"But I have promised," replied Joseph, "that I cannot give you the money unless the other two are present."

"Yes," said O'Flynn, "but the other two cannot come. They are busy negotiating with the owner of the cargo. They have agreed that you should hand over the money."

Joseph was a man who naturally believed what people said. So he went to the strongroom, took out the money, and handed it to O'Flynn.

Six months later O'Leary and O'Connell arrived at Joseph's house, expecting to meet O'Flynn there. When Joseph explained what had happened they were furious – with O'Flynn for his deceit, and with Joseph for his folly. So they decided to take Joseph to court, in the hope of forcing him to pay for his folly from his own money.

At court the judge asked Joseph what answer he had to the charge made against him.

"No answer, sir," Joseph replied, sobbing gently.

"Joseph accepts that he owes you the money," the judge said, turning to O'Leary and O'Connell. "But by the terms of your agreement with him, he can only pay you when all three of you are present together. So bring O'Flynn to court, and you shall receive your money."

THE SHOUTING HERMIT

A visitor in Connacht came to a village which was at the foot of a steep hill. The village people told the visitor about the hermit who lived on the hill.

"We hear him talk and argue with God," they said. "He is pleading with God on our behalf. It is because of his prayers that our crops grow so well, and our cows yield such creamy milk."

So the visitor climbed the hill to meet this remarkable hermit.

"Do you truly talk and argue with God?" the visitor asked.

"When I first came here," the hermit replied, "I was afraid, especially at night. So I began shouting to make me feel brave."

"Then what happened?"

"The people heard my shouting, and started to bring me food. And so long as I carry on shouting, they continue to bring me food. Surely God is a wonderful provider!"

FIVE

RICHES
AND POVERTY

FOLLOWING CHRIST

When I started to follow Christ
Men of the world no longer saw me.
Their eyes looked at me,
But their gaze passed through me.

I no longer wanted wealth,
So they regarded me as mad.
I no longer wanted power,
So they regarded me as stupid.

"Why should we speak to such a man?"
They said to one another.
"Let us just ignore him."
So they did.

WEALTH AS LOAN

When I give alms to the poor,
Let me not congratulate myself.
Let there be no pride in my act.

The wealth I possess is on loan;
God has made me its steward.
I am God's hands and God's heart.

Let my love for others be God's love;
Let my pity for the needy be God's pity;
Let my alms be received as God's gift.

FLIES ROUND A FLAME

People gather round the wealthy man like flies
    round a flame,
When he boasts they praise him, when he lies
    they believe him.

When he jokes they laugh, when he's serious
    they frown.
"He is wise and handsome," they say in his
    hearing.

I would hate to be rich and surrounded by flies.
I want friends to prick my pride, and speak
    the truth.
If ever I grow rich, I shall hide my wealth.
Then my friends will still be real, and their
    voices honest.

But if I hide my wealth, I shall be lying.
Better to remain poor.

FALSE GLORY AND FALSE FRIENDS

Does "wealthy" mean "wise" and "free"?
Does "poor" mean "foolish" and "enslaved"?

That is what the world imagines.
It thinks wealth brings glory, honor and cheer.
It thinks wealth brings friends flocking to the door.
But is such glory truly glorious?
Are such friends truly friendly?

Does "wealthy" mean "foolish" and "enslaved"?
Does "poor" mean "wise" and "free"?

That is what the gospel teaches.

NO HERDS OR FLOCKS

I own no herds of cattle, or flocks of sheep.
I have no horses in stalls, or geese in pens.
I have no jewels or gold in my house.
I have no wheat or corn in my barn.

Some show pity, others contempt.
But I feel free.

My rich neighbors with herds and flocks are
       always anxious.
Daily they count their stock.
My rich neighbors with gold and jewels are
       always anxious.
Nightly they count their money.

I love them in their folly.
I want to lift their burden.

THE WORLD AND THE CHURCH

In the world people get what they pay for.
So the rich, who have much to spend,
Have much to enjoy;
While the poor, who have little to spend,
Have little to enjoy.

In church they should get what they need.
So the rich, who at present have much,
Should give much and receive little;
While the poor, who at present have little,
Should give little, and receive much.

Let the world flourish and prosper;
And the church set right its wrongs.

DESIRE AND GRASP

Those who own land are often greedy for more.
Those who own nothing are often content.

It is not wealth which brings contentment.
Nor poverty which brings misery.
What matters is the gap between desire and grasp.
The smaller the gap, the happier the mind.

THE GLAD BEGGAR

Let those with well-paid jobs –
Merchants, lawyers and the like –
Be grateful for their wealth.

Let those with food on the table,
And a roof above their heads,
Rejoice in their security.

But I am glad to be a beggar.
One day I go hungry and cold,
The next I have food and warmth.

I have learned never to be bitter,
Even when my luck is down;
And to praise God when luck is up.

Praise God for what I enjoy.
Smile at what I lack.

THE BLESSINGS OF KINDNESS

May those who oppress the poor be cursed.
May no butter crown their milk;
May their ducks yield no down;
May fire in summer burn their crops;
May midges eat their flesh.

May those who feed the poor be blessed.
May their milk be thick with cream;
May they sleep on softest pillows;
May their crops be heavy with grain;
May they always be hale and strong.

THE RICH MAN AND DEATH

Rich man   I have never done anything which, in my opinion, deserves great punishment. I have never committed murder; I have never stolen; I have been faithful to my wife. I have lived a blameless life.

Death   How are you so certain that your life is blameless?

Rich man   You do not need to take my word. Talk to the other men of property in my neighborhood. They all hold me in the highest esteem.

Death   Do you take pleasure in this esteem? Has winning the respect of others been the motive for your blameless life?

Rich man   If I say "yes" you will accuse me of the sin of pride. If I say "no" you will call me dishonest.

Death   Do you think that merely being free of blame is sufficient?

Rich man In addition to committing no sins, I have done many good things. I have given lodging to tramps, and food to beggars. I have never turned away a poor man at my gate.

Death Have those who have received your bounty been grateful?

Rich man I have demanded gratitude. I will give once to a man who does not thank me, but not twice.

Death Why should they thank you?

Rich man Because I have worked hard for my wealth, while they do nothing.

Death And who do you thank for the wealth you have received?

Rich man Again you are trying to trick me. You want me to say that I thank no one, because I deserve my wealth. But I will not fall for your trick. I go to church every Sunday and offer thanks for God's blessings.

Death	So why do you not ask the poor to thank God for what you give them?
Rich man	You are too clever for me. I can see that you lure innocent people into saying things they do not intend, so you can gain power over their souls.
Death	Have you not become rich by luring innocent people into giving you things they do not intend, so you can gain power over their bodies?

RACE FOR LAND

Every week a man came to the King of Connacht, and begged the king to grant him land.

"If I had land of my own," the man would say, "then I would be truly happy."

Eventually the king grew so weary of this man's pleadings that he gave in.

"I will grant you," said the king, "all the land you can walk around in one day, from dawn till dusk. But you must complete the circle by returning to the place where you started."

The man was delighted. The next morning he rose early. The king had also risen early and was waiting for him. As the sun rose, the man set off. The king noted where he had started.

The man ran as fast as he could. When he got tired he walked for a time; and as soon as he got his breath back he started to run again.

As the sun rose to the top of the sky, the man felt very pleased with the great distance he had covered. But as the sun began to descend, his legs grew heavier and his pace slackened.

When the sun touched the western horizon the man was still a long way from his starting-point. He could see the king in the distance waiting for him.

The man tried to go faster. But the harder he tried, the heavier his legs became. And as the sun sank below the horizon, the man collapsed. The king ran to him, and wiped his face with a cool, wet cloth. The man opened his eyes.

"I have been defeated by my own greed," the man said, and lay back in the king's arms.

THE SOUND OF MONEY

A wandering preacher arrived in a town. It was market day, so all the people were busy buying and selling. It was so noisy that people could hardly hear what they were saying.

The preacher stood up on a bench in the middle of the market square; and at the top of his voice he began to preach about Jesus Christ. Most people ignored him. A few turned around and told him to keep quiet.

"On market day," they shouted, "we're too busy buying and selling to worry about religion. Come back on Sunday."

So the preacher took a large silver coin from his pocket, lifted it high above his head, and let it fall on the stone cobbles beneath. It landed with a loud clink. At the sound of a coin dropping on the ground, the crowd fell silent, and turned towards the preacher.

"You have ears to hear the sound of money," the preacher said. "Why do you not have ears for the gospel as well – when you most need it?"

The people now felt ashamed. They remained silent for a full 20 minutes, while the preacher spoke to them. Only then did they resume their business.

NATURAL TREASURE

Paddy grew the finest gooseberries, black currants and red currants in the whole country. He had three fields of fruit bushes, and every day he walked round the bushes with a hoe, taking out any weeds which were growing. So the bushes had all the goodness of the soil to themselves. By the middle of each summer they were heavy with large, juicy fruit.

But sadly, Paddy was not as good at raising children as he was at raising fruit. His two sons were known as the laziest young men in the country. They spent all day drinking, eating and chatting with friends; they never lifted a finger to help their father. As the years passed, Paddy became increasingly anxious about his sons' laziness.

"When I am dead and gone," he would say to his neighbors, "all my fruit bushes will become overgrown with weeds, and my sons will starve."

Living a short distance from the village in a small cave was a hermit, renowned for his wily wisdom. Finally Paddy decided to visit this hermit, to ask advice. After he had heard Paddy's story, the hermit sat for a few moments in silence, stroking his long, white beard. At last the hermit rose up, patted Paddy on the shoulder, and assured him that he would teach the two lazy sons to work. Then the hermit left his hut, and went to see the young men.

"I have something very important to tell you," he said to them. "I happen to know that in those fields of fruit bushes there is great treasure. It will be enough to feed and clothe you for the rest of your lives."

It was now September. From then until Christmas the two sons went out into the fields each day searching for treasure.

They dug round every fruit bush, turning over the earth, in the hope of finding a casket full of gold. But by Christmas Eve they had found nothing. So they went to the hermit, and accused him of deceiving them.

"I haven't deceived you," the hermit replied, with a grin.

"You must keep searching. I promise that by next September you will have found the treasure."

The sons refused to believe him.

"Very well, then," the hermit continued, "I will make a bargain with you. If by September you have not found enough treasure to buy food and clothing for you for the rest of your lives, I will share of whatever I receive with you. But if you do find treasure, you must share it with the poor in this village."

The brothers agreed. So they continued to dig the fields, turning over the earth between the fruit bushes. Paddy watched with great satisfaction, pleased that while his sons searched for treasure, no weeds would grow. Thus by the middle of summer the bushes were again heavy with large and juicy fruit. The hermit came to the fields to see the two sons.

"Ah," he exclaimed, looking at the fruit bushes, "I see you have found your treasure."

At first the two sons could not think what he meant. Then it dawned on them. Over the next few weeks the hermit helped them to pick the treasure. Half they sold in the market; and the other half they gave to the poor.

And from then on the two brothers continued to work hard in the fields. Each year they again sold half the crop, and gave away the rest. And, as the hermit had prophesied, the money they got was quite sufficient to feed and clothe them for the rest of their lives.

OWNING BEAUTY

The richest man in the town had a collection of fabulous jewels, which he kept locked away in a safe. One day the priest called.

"I have heard you have in your safe the most fabulous jewels," the priest said. "Would you allow me to see them?"

"It would be a pleasure," the rich man said. "I haven't looked at them myself for some years, so I too will enjoy seeing them."

The rich man opened the safe, took out the gold box filled with jewels, and then spread the jewels on a table. Both the priest and the rich man stared at them, awestruck by their beauty. Then the rich man put the jewels back in the gold box, returned the gold box to the safe, and locked the safe door.

"Thank you for giving me those jewels," the priest said.

"But I haven't given them to you," the rich man indignantly replied. "They belong to me."

"I have had as much pleasure as you from looking at the jewels," the priest replied. "So there is no difference between us – except that you have the expense and anxiety of buying them and looking after them."

That day the rich man gave away one jewel to every household in the town. There were just enough – with one left over for himself.

THE YOUNG THIEF

A young thief, who was very successful at his evil occupation, felt increasingly troubled in his conscience. So he went to visit a wise old priest. To his surprise the priest did not tell him to give up thieving at once.

"I want you to find other young men to join you," the priest said. "Then you must teach them to rob from the rich people of our land, and to give to the poor."

"But surely thieving from anyone is wrong," the young thief said. "I expected you to make me confess my sins, and repent."

"God can use even the most wicked actions for good purposes," the priest replied.

So the young thief gathered round him a small army of other young men. And together they began stealing gold and silver from all the castles and palaces in the land; then they gave what they had stolen to the poor. They were so successful that gradually the poor became richer, and the rich became poorer. Finally, in despair, the rich people came themselves to see the wise old priest, to ask for help.

"If you promise to use your wealth for the good of all," the priest said, "I will tell the young thieves to stop."

In this way the land enjoyed a period of justice and prosperity, such that it had not known before – and has not known since.

SIX

PLEASURE
AND PAIN

SHARING PLEASURE

Consider those who find no pleasure in helping
  others.
The darkest night, with neither stars nor
  moonlight,
Is brighter than their brightest day.

Consider those who find no pleasure in
  receiving help.
The coldest winter, when the earth is hard as stone,
Is warmer than their icy hearts.

There is no pleasure in seeking pleasure for
  yourself.
The only pleasure lies in sharing pleasure.

WHEN BLOOD SURGES

When you are excited, and feel the blood in
    your veins
Surging like a tide in spring,
What is it that excites you?

Is it a horse on which you have placed a bet
Running first in the field?

Is it a woman whose beauty fills your eyes
Smiling and winking at you?

Or is it the stories of saints from long ago
Who gave their lives for God?

When your blood surges, your heart follows.

RISING IN THE MORNING

When you rise in the morning, what fills
    your head?

Are you thinking of food and drink, the pleasures
    ahead?
Are you planning the work you must do, the
    labor ahead?
Are you fearful of snares and dangers, the evils
    ahead?
Are you hopeful of all you'll achieve, the
    successes ahead?

Let all those worldly thoughts swirl in your mind;
Then let them flush away, like dirt in a river.
Empty your head; let your brain be at peace.
Quietly, calmly, serenely – offer the day to God.

THANKING GOD

I thank God for this horsehair mattress.
I thank God for this down-filled pillow,
And also for this warm, wool blanket.

I thank God for the gift of sleep.
I thank God for peace of mind,
And also for soothing my limbs.

I thank God for the nights awake.
I thank God when my mind keeps turning,
And also for a restless body.

The nights of sleep are a joy.
The nights awake are a trial.
Through both my faith is deepened.

HEAVEN NOW

If I were in heaven, I would play my harp,
And sing songs of praise with the angels.
If I were in heaven, I would dance with joy,
And fill the air with laughter.

Let earth be like heaven, and people like angels;
Let all sing songs of praise.
Don't wait to die, enjoy heaven now;
Don't argue or cavil – just dance.

HEAVEN ON EARTH

To the person that sleeps on horsehair
A down mattress is heaven.

To the person that lives on spuds
Roast beef is heaven.

To the person in a rough wool tunic
A silk shirt is heaven.

To the person with a nagging spouse
Quiet solitude is heaven.

To the person living alone
A loving spouse is heaven.

Let the Lord give us what we need,
And let heaven stay in heaven.

THE DOCTOR AND THE PRIEST

The two people commanding the greatest respect
Are the doctor and the priest.
The doctor cures our physical ailments,
The priest heals our spiritual ones.

This tells us that our deepest desire
Is to be healthy in body and soul.

Yet some want the doctor, not the priest.
They care for the body, but not the soul.
Some want the priest, not the doctor.
They care for the soul, not the body.

This tells us that our desire can be twisted.
Good health involves both body and soul.

SEXUAL PLEASURE

Sexual pleasure lasts only for a few short moments,
Yet people have ruined themselves in pursuit of it.

Men have abandoned good wives for the sake
of lust.
They have deserted their children in the quest for
pleasure.
They have made themselves poor in the madness
of desire,
Neglecting their crops for a beautiful woman.

When God created sex, God fixed a vast chasm
Between desire and pleasure, between
expectation and achievement.

Was this God's trick, to give God pleasure?
Let us laugh at the chasm, but never try to cross it.

SIMPLE LIVING

Where did you sleep last night;
And what were your dreams?
Did you sleep in a warm, soft bed
And dream of the people you love?

What did you eat last night;
And what did you drink?
Did you eat good, simple food
And drink mead and ale and wine?

Good sleep, sweet dreams;
Good food, sweet drink.
How simple are life's pleasures;
How hard they are to find.

SMILING LIKE A CHILD

Many priests wear faces of gloom,
Believing that gloom is holy.
They recite the prayers in hushed tones,
Believing that hush is holy.

Yet the gospel of Christ is joyful.
He wants to bring heaven to earth.
He invites us to pray like children,
Crying and laughing and sighing.

A priest should smile like a child,
And laugh and cry like a babe.
A priest should learn to pray like a child,
Crying and laughing and sighing.

NO GRASS GROWS

I roam where no grass will grow.
The bees make no honey, the cows are dry.
At night the moon withholds her borrowed light;
By day the sun is shrouded in dark clouds.
The wheat and barley wither on the stalk,
Fruits shrivel before they ripen.

God has withdrawn life's blessings
And has decided to test my faith.
Will I continue to love and trust God
Even in this bleak, harsh wilderness?
God does not bless me, I want to curse God.
Let my curses melt into blessings.

A BAD BACK

From years of digging and living,
From years of plowing and sowing,
From years of reaping and threshing,
My back is in permanent pain.

At night when the pain prevents slumber,
I curse those years of toil.
In daylight when the pain prevents work,
I pray to God for strength.

In those few moments when the pain eases,
My joy in life is immense – praise God.
After those moments when the pain returns,
I long for heaven's joy – praise God.

REASONS FOR TREMBLING

There are four reasons why a person may tremble.
The person may be frightened, and tremble
    with fear.
The person may be ill, and tremble with a fever.
The person may be angry, and tremble with rage.
The person may be in love, and tremble with
    passion.

Fear, fever, rage, passion –
All are created by God.
What makes us frightened,
What makes us ill,
What makes us angry,
What makes us love –
On these matters we have some choice,
On these we must seek God's grace.

THE TONGUE

How easily I hurt people with my tongue –
Like a whip lashing at their soul,
Like a spear piercing their heart,
Like a boulder crushing their mind.

I never intend to misuse my tongue.
Yet the bad and evil habits of my spirit
Find expression unwittingly through my mouth.
Let my spirit grow gentle – then my tongue
    will be kind.

WELCOME FRIDAY

Welcome Friday, I love this day.
The day our Lord was crucified.
A day for quiet reflection,
A day of earnest prayer,
A day to remember one's sins,
A day to beg forgiveness,
A day to abstain from good food,
A day to shun fine wine,
A day to turn towards goodness,
A day to plan acts of charity,
A day to give thanks for all God's blessings.

WELCOME SUNDAY

Welcome Sunday, I love this day.
The day our Lord rose to life.
A day of joy and rest,
A day to laugh with family and friends,
A day to play with children,
A day to enjoy the beauty of Nature,
A day to sit at home by the fire,
A day to tell the stories of old,
A day to sing and to dance,
A day to worship the God who made us,
A day to give thanks for all God's blessings.

A SUMMER MORNING

A summer morning; my eyes are open.
The sun is bright: I see clouds scudding by,
Birds in the air, flowers in the meadow,
Bees in the flowers, cows eating grass.

A summer morning; my eyes are closed.
The sun is warm: I hear birds singing,
Bees buzzing, cows munching.
I feel wind on my cheek, smell flowers beneath me.

All my senses are alive.
Thank God for beauty.

A MEADOW IN JUNE

I walk through a meadow in June.
Wild flowers stroke my legs,
Red and yellow petals caress me,
The dew on the grass washes me.

Is each tiny flower an angel?
Is each petal an angelic finger?
Are the angels cleansing me of sin?
Are the angels my lovers and friends?

Here and now God is present;
Here and now heaven is on earth;
Here and now eternity is present;
Here and now joy is infinite.

THE PRIEST AND THE FISHERMAN

Priest	Why are you just sitting on the sand by your boat?
Fisherman	Because it's a warm sunny day.
Priest	You should be out at sea catching fish instead of just lying around.
Fisherman	Why should I catch more fish?
Priest	So you can make more money.
Fisherman	Why should I make more money?
Priest	So you can buy another boat, and employ more fishermen, and catch more fish.
Fisherman	Why should I do that?
Priest	So you can make even more money.
Fisherman	What good would that do me?
Priest	After working hard and making money, you could sit back and relax.
Fisherman	That's just what I'm doing now.

THE GRIEVING WIDOW

The old couple who lived in a cottage on the edge of the village were envied for the happiness of their marriage. They never quarrelled and were always affectionate to one another.

Sadly, after 34 years of this happiness, the husband became ill and died.

The wife was overcome with grief. Her children tried to console her, but to no avail. Her neighbors tried to console her, but with similar lack of success. Weeks and months went by, and still the woman was grieving; tears fell down her cheeks from morning until night.

Then a holy man came to the village. People told him about the woman, and asked him to try to help her. The holy man went to the woman's house. Although he was dressed only in a rough woollen tunic, the holy man had on his left index finger a gold ring with an emerald set within it. He took off the ring, and handed it to the woman.

"I want you to give this to the family which has no sorrows," the man said.

The woman set off in search of such a family. She visited every home in the district, and talked to the people. Finally she returned home, and gave back the ring to the holy man. Her grief had gone.

SEVEN

PEACE AND CONFLICT

MY ENEMIES

From the enemies of my land,
From the enemies of my faith,
From the enemies of all that is good and true,
May the cross of Christ preserve me.

May the cross bring us peace,
May the cross bring us love,
May the cross preserve us from all evil and lies,
And carry us to the safety of heaven.

TEST OF FELLOWSHIP

People have always argued and disagreed.
On every matter there have been two sides.

Christ urged us to love and be united.
On every matter he wanted perfect harmony.

Christians have continued to argue and disagree.
On matters of doctrine there have been two sides.

Can we argue and remain united?
Can we disagree and remain in harmony?

That is the true test of fellowship.

OFFICERS AND SOLDIERS

The man who rides at the front of an army
Is admired by his officers, yet also envied.
Others close behind are waiting for him to fall
So they can push themselves forward.

Yet the soldiers who march on foot envy no one.
They have no prospect of promotion, so they rest
    content.
When one is wounded others carry him.
All are equal, so all are friends.

The gospel makes everyone a soldier,
And every soldier an officer.
All are followers, and all are leaders.
All command, and all obey.

THE DECEIT OF ANGER

A man is angry with his child.
He goes to the wood to fetch a stick.
He grabs his child and beats his body.
Who has he served: the child or himself?

A woman is angry with her neighbor.
She is convinced her neighbor has done wrong.
She shouts curses, she condemns her in public.
Who has she served: the neighbor or herself?

Anger is a deceitful master.
It tells us we are right
Even when we hurt people we love.

MY SHOULDERS ARE WIDE

My shoulders are wide and strong,
My arms ripple with muscle,
My legs are as large as tree trunks,
My back is like a towering wall.

Yet faced with temptation I am weak,
As weak as a tiny twig.
When I want an object I grab it,
When I want a woman I demand her.

I abuse my physical strength
To indulge my moral weakness.
Let my muscles shrivel to nothing
And my spirit grow strong as an oak.

HUNTER AND HUNTED

I love hunting wild animals and birds.
I enjoy shooting an arrow into the air,
And watching my prey slump to the ground.
I love eating the meat I have killed.

But I hate being hunted by my enemies.
I fear the wild ones with swords and cudgels;
And flee from those with lances and spears.
I dread seeing my friends fall in battle.

Should I do to birds and animals
What I hate being done to me?
Or should I treat God's creatures
As I want others to treat me?

WEARY OF WAR

I am weary of fighting my enemies.
All my life I have strived to win.
I can look back on many famous victories
And a few miserable defeats.

Yet winning has lost its taste;
Victory brings no sense of glory.
Instead of fighting I should have been smiling –
Winning friends instead of battles.

If an enemy now attacks me,
I shall die rather than fight.
The Lord turned death into life,
Mortal defeat into glorious triumph.

THE SPIRITUAL SHIELD

Imagine a shield which could protect me
Even from a humming gnat,
Even from a ray of sunlight,
Even from the sound of thunder.

Let the spiritual shield which protects me from evil
Be as good.

I want my soul to be free from
Even the smallest sinful emotion –
Every kind of evil.

TRUE STRENGTH

If Christ and the largest person in the world
Were locked in combat;
And Christ were to knock the largest person
Onto the muddy turf;
Would that convince you that Christ is truly
    strong?

If Christ and the cleverest person in the world
Were locked in debate;
And Christ were to outwit the cleverest person
In verbal battle;
Would that convince you that Christ is truly wise?

Yet Christ told us to turn the other cheek;
And he allowed himself to be killed by cleverer
    people.
He was weak and he was foolish.
In this lay his strength and wisdom.

AN UNTAMED HORSE

My heart is like an untamed horse.

For a while the horse is calm and steady,
Then suddenly it starts to buck.
For a while peace rules in my breast,
Then sinful desire overwhelms me.

A good rider can tame the horse,
So it always obeys commands.
The challenge of life is to tame the heart
So it always obeys the will.

ENEMIES INTO FRIENDS

It is better to roam the world
With a stick in your hand for pulling fruit
    from trees,
Than a sword at your side for killing enemies.

God has put fruit on trees to sustain our bodies,
And love in our hearts to make enemies into
    friends.

A LIGHT IN THE DARKNESS

Jonathan and Thomas were constantly arguing. They were next door neighbors; and whenever they saw each other they found something rude to say. One day Jonathan would criticize Thomas for allowing his cattle to lean over the fence and eat grass from Jonathan's field. The next day Thomas would be angry with Jonathan because nettles from Jonathan's land were spreading onto Thomas's land. Their two wives were close friends, and they longed for Jonathan and Thomas also to be friends.

Eventually, one winter, the two long-suffering women decided that they could stand it no longer. "Christmas will soon be here," they said to their husbands. "It is supposed to be the season of peace and goodwill. Surely you can learn to be at peace with each other and stop arguing."

But the very next day Thomas accused Jonathan of shoveling snow onto his land – and a fierce argument arose. So their wives went to the local priest to see if he could find an answer. Father Kevin was an old man, with a bald head and a long white beard. After he had heard the two wives pour out their troubles, he sat in silence, scratching his bald pate and stroking his beard. Then, without saying a word, he rose up and went out to see the two men.

"I want you to enter a competition with me on Christmas Eve," the priest began. "It will provide entertainment for the whole village. The competition is this. We will divide the barn outside my cottage into three equal parts. Between dawn and dusk we will see which of us can fill our part the fullest using anything we like. If either of you wins, you can take all the fruit and vegetables which grow in my garden over the next year. If I win, you must promise never to argue again, and instead learn to be friends."

Jonathan and Thomas thought they had nothing to lose, so they agreed to the competition. At dawn on Christmas Eve the whole village had gathered round the barn. And as soon as the sun was visible above the eastern horizon, Jonathan and Thomas began rushing round the village collecting anything they could to fill their parts of the barn – bales of straw, old buckets, sacks of potatoes, and whatever else they could carry. But Father Kevin was nowhere to be seen.

At lunchtime Jonathan and Thomas were still busily trying to fill their parts of the barn. And Father Kevin was still nowhere to be seen. A few hours later, as the sun began to set below the western horizon, Jonathan and Thomas had both filled their parts of the barn almost to the roof. But Father Kevin's part was still completely empty. Finally, as the last rays of the sun were fading, Father Kevin came out of his cottage carrying an unlit candle. He walked into the barn, and placed the candle in the middle. He spoke the verse from the opening chapter of St. John's gospel: "The light of Christ shines in the darkness, and the darkness cannot overcome it." Then he knelt down and lit the candle.

In the darkness of Christmas Eve, its light filled the whole barn, shining right up into the rafters of the roof. A great cheer arose, as everyone realized that Father Kevin had won the competition. Jonathan and Thomas stepped forward and, standing over the candle, shook hands. And from that Christmas onwards they were the firmest friends.

TRUST AMONG THIEVES

A man was traveling from the east of the country to the west. The route passed through a remote region of marshes and lakes, where few people lived, and where travelers were often robbed. As he reached this region he saw a large house.

"I will ask the owner of this house to look over my purse of gold and silver," the man said to himself, "and I will collect it on my return. Then it will be safe from robbers."

So he knocked on the door of the house. The owner welcomed him warmly and agreed to look after his gold and silver until his return. The man continued his journey. A few miles further on, with lakes and marshes all around, the man was attacked by robbers. They took the few coins he had in his pocket, and then went on their way.

A few days later the man was returning from the west. He knocked on the door of the large house. The owner opened it, and there in the front room were the robbers who had attacked him. He realized at once that the owner of the house was their chief.

"Come in," the owner said, "and collect your purse of gold and silver."

"But why are you giving back my purse, when you are the chief among thieves?"

"Because you trusted me," came the reply. "If there were no trust, these robbers would not come and share their spoils with me. All who trust me, I trust in return."

STARTING A FIGHT

A holy man wandered into a village. He met the village priest in the marketplace. The priest began to show off about his ministry.

"I have been here ten years," the priest said. "When I arrived there were fights in the village almost every day. But thanks to my Christian preaching and teaching, we have had no fights for a whole year."

"I congratulate you," the holy man replied. "But beware of thinking that you have driven out the urge to fight by your preaching."

"Rest assured," the priest said smugly, "I have these people under my control."

The holy man went into a shop selling honey. He began smearing a large amount of honey on a wall. Soon great swarms of flies had descended on the honey. The larger insects arrived to catch the flies. A cat arrived, and tried to catch the larger insects. A dog passed by, and, seeing the cat, attacked it.

A youth saw the dog attack the cat, and hit the dog with a stick. The owner of the dog was furious, and punched the youth. The youth returned the punch. Quickly a crowd gathered to watch the fight, some shouting in support of the youth, others in support of the dog owner.

"To keep the peace," the holy man said to the priest, "requires constant vigilance. Your work is never done."

And the holy man went on his way.

EIGHT

WISDOM
AND FOLLY

GOOD ADVICE

My father gave me good advice.
I heard what he said, but did not listen to his words.
My father gave me many blessings.
But I was indifferent to both his blessings and
    his curses.

Now my father has died, and I have lost him.
I am old enough to listen, but he no longer speaks.
I want him to bless me, but his hand is cold
    and limp.
I can never get him back.

Instead I shall turn to God for counsel,
And I shall beg God to guide my actions.
Goodbye father; welcome Father.

THE STONES OF MY HOUSE

The stones of my house are my witnesses.
They have seen all my good deeds and bad.
They have watched over my joys and my sorrows.
They have observed me in every mood.

If they could speak, they could tell my story.
Am I glad they are dumb?
Or would I like them to talk?
Am I ashamed or proud of my life?

These stones are the eyes of God.
Whenever I look on those stones,
Let me remember that God looks on me.

NEVER MOCK

Never mock what others say.
Perhaps their words are full of nonsense.
Perhaps they are trying to puff themselves up.
Perhaps they like hearing the sound of their voices.
Perhaps they are trying to deceive their hearers.
Perhaps they are foolish and dim.
Perhaps they are more clever than wise.
Yet amidst the useless clay
You may find jewels beyond price.
The word of God is in every heart,
And can speak through every voice.

CONTENT WITH YOURSELF

There are old women who wear young clothes.
Their faces are wrinkled and their breasts sag,
But they wear the bright garments of youth.

Who are they trying to fool?
Do they think others look only at their clothes,
And ignore the grey hairs and rattling teeth?
Or are they fooling themselves?

Be content with what you are.
If young, rejoice in youth.
If old, rejoice in age.
If clever, rejoice in wit.
If slow, rejoice in caution.
If handsome, rejoice in beauty.
If plain, rejoice in simplicity.
Whatever you are, give thanks to God.

SPIRITUAL SAFETY

If we wander far away to lonely places,
There is no one to help us when danger comes.

If we wander far from the love of our friends,
There is no one to help us when the devil comes.

For your bodily safety stay close to home,
So friends are near to protect you.

For your spiritual safety stay close to home,
So friends are near to protect you.

AS OTHERS SEE YOU

Do you see yourself as others see you?
Do you recognize the virtues and abilities that
    others do?
Do you acknowledge your faults and vices?

Or do you underestimate yourself, talk yourself
    down,
And so let your abilities go to waste?
Or do you overestimate yourself, talk yourself up,
And so denigrate the abilities of others?

You cannot know the answers to these questions.
But listen carefully, and you may learn.

REFLECTED GLORY

Do you judge yourself by the company you keep?
Do you enjoy the reflected glory of others?

When you consort with kings, you think yourself
   powerful.
When you talk with scholars, you think yourself
   wise.
When you sit with monks, you think yourself holy.
When you chatter with knights, you think yourself
   strong.

Yet if others judged themselves by your company,
What would they think?

CITY AND COUNTRY

The country has its ways:
Rugged, simple and tough.
The city has its ways:
Smooth, refined and easy.

Country people envy the city,
But are proud of their country ways.
City people despise the country,
Yet yearn for rustic quiet.

Could not every village become a small city,
And every city be sprinkled with green fields?

A PERSON WHO STUTTERS

A person who stutters is not to be despised.
A person with a cleft palate is not to be ridiculed.
Most of what is said clearly is ignorant nonsense.
So it is better to mangle the words.

And even when words of wisdom are uttered,
A stutter or a cleft palate are an advantage.
The listener is forced to concentrate hard,
So the wisdom enters their head.

FAME

Long ago I was famous.
People called me golden-tongued.
They flocked to hear me preach.
I was the finest speaker in the land.

But fame withers faster than wealth.
I lost my skill at speaking.
I lost my desire to inspire.
Soon the people forgot me.

I thought I was serving God.
In truth I was serving pride.
I thought myself full of joy.
In truth my soul was rotten.

Thank God for taking fame away.
Thank God for giving humility.

ONE KEY, ONE DOOR

We have one key for each lock; one key opens one door.

Have one prayer for each good intention; one prayer brings one answer.

Have one act of charity for each need you see; one act yields one fruit.

Have one fear for each sin; one fear gives protection from one evil deed.

Have one thought for each piece of wisdom; one thought leads to good habit.

THE WISE FOOL

Rafferty was the richest man in the town. He lived in a large house on the east side of the town, while his mother lived in a small cottage on the west side. His mother was very old, and gradually became so weak that she needed someone attending her all the time. Rafferty did not wish to attend her himself. So each night he sent a young man to sit by her bedside.

"I will pay any young man who attends my mother five silver coins each night," he said. "At dawn the young man must bring news of her condition. The one who tells me she has died will himself die."

For a whole year seven young men – one for each night of the week – sat by her bedside. One of these young men was a simpleton called Jack – he was known as the town fool. In the middle of each night Rafferty sent his manservant to check that the young man was at the bedside, and that his mother was still alive.

After a year the mother grew so weak that death was imminent. And on the night she died Jack was at her bedside. He was very frightened, because he knew that the manservant would soon come; and seeing the old woman was dead, the manservant would drag him back to Rafferty, who would kill him. So the fool took the knife which the old woman used to cut meat and bread; and he stood behind the door. When the manservant came in, Jack caught him from behind, and cut off his head.

Jack was now worried that, if he tried to escape, Rafferty would send men to catch him. So he decided to go to Rafferty's house, to compel him to spare his life.

He arrived at Rafferty's house as dawn was breaking. Rafferty came out, with a sword in his hand, to see Jack.

"Why has my manservant not returned?" asked Rafferty gruffly.

"Because I knocked off his hat; and he does

not want to walk the street without a hat. Will you forgive me for knocking off the hat?"

"Of course I forgive such a trivial thing," Rafferty replied.

"And his head came off as well," Jack added. But since Rafferty had already forgiven him, he could not punish him.

"Have you other news to bring?" Rafferty asked.

"I have," said Jack. "God's brightness is over the earth."

"That is because the sun has risen, you fool," said Rafferty. "What other news?"

"The house where you were reared is now quiet," said Jack.

"You mean my mother has died."

"Ah," replied Jack, "you are telling yourself this news. So you cannot punish me."

Jack then skipped into the center of town. And that is the origin of the old Irish saying, "There's wisdom in being a fool."

THE SHEEP AND THE PURSE

A man was walking along a road taking a sheep to market. The sheep was walking behind him on a tether.

A thief came up behind him, cut the tether and stole the sheep. When the man realized what had happened he was very upset. He ran off in search of the thief and the sheep.

Eventually he came to a well. At the side of the well sat a man, apparently in despair. Although the owner of the sheep did not know it, the man was the thief – who had already sold the sheep.

"Why are you in such despair?"

"I have dropped my purse in the well," the thief replied. "It contains 100 pieces of silver. If you could get it back for me, I would happily give you 20 pieces."

The man, who was a good diver, was delighted, thinking that 20 pieces of silver was worth far more than the sheep he had lost. So he took off his clothes, and dived in the well.

While he was under water, the thief took his clothes and ran off.

THE PRIEST AND THE BEGGAR

Priest   What are you doing with a pig on a tether, sitting at the side of the road?

Beggar   What are you doing with a rein in your hand, sitting on a black horse?

Priest   And how long have you been here?

Beggar   I've been here as long as the road.

Priest   Whose are those little piglets?

Beggar   They are the pig's.

Priest   I know that, but I'm asking you who is the master of the piglets.

Beggar   Nature is their master – Nature teaches them to eat and to drink, to walk and to run.

Priest   All right. Who is your master?

Beggar   My master is my mistress's husband, as good a man as you could find here.

Priest   So who is your mistress?

Beggar   My master's wife. Everyone knows that.

Priest   Let me ask you something easy, where

you can give me an answer which will help me. Where is Patrick O'Donnell living?

Beggar Point your arm up, and follow it until it aches. Then follow your nose. If you miss his house, blame your guides.

Priest You're an impudent man. What is your trade?

Beggar I have a good trade. I show people the way to heaven.

Priest That is my trade: I show people the way to heaven.

Beggar How can you show people the way to heaven? You don't even know the way to Patrick O'Donnell's house.

Priest I'm beaten. Here's a silver coin for you.

Beggar Thank you. It's a pity a fool like you doesn't come this way every day.

THE MONSTER MARROW

The people of a certain village were very foolish. One year they grew marrows in a field near the village. And one of these marrows grew so vast that the people thought it must be dangerous. They called it a monster and they were so frightened that they would not go into the field to pick the other marrows.

A traveling preacher arrived in the village, and they told him about the monster. He looked across the field, and saw that it was only an outsized marrow. So he offered to kill the monster for them. He went into the field with a knife, cut a slice from the marrow, and began to eat it. The foolish villagers thought that any man who could attack a monster with such lack of fear must himself be a monster. So they chased him out of the village with pitchforks.

A few days later, another traveling preacher came to the village and they showed him the monster marrow as well. Instead of offering to kill the monster, he agreed with them that it could indeed be dangerous. And he tiptoed away from the field, as if he himself was terrified. In this way he won their trust.

He spent many weeks in the village. And by his gentle teaching he taught the people that everything around them is created by God, so they should be frightened of nothing – even outsized marrows. And gradually their folly turned to wisdom – and their fear to trust.

FLOUR AND SALT

A mother sent her foolish son to buy flour and salt, telling him not to mix the two. He took a dish to carry his purchases, and went to the shop. The shopkeeper measured out the flour, and put it in the dish. Then he began to measure out the salt.

"Be careful not to mix the salt and the flour," the foolish son said.

"So where shall I put the salt?" the shopkeeper asked.

"In here," the foolish son said. He turned the bowl upside down, to show the flat bottom on which the salt could be laid. The flour spilled onto the floor. The foolish son returned home, with the salt safely on the bottom of the bowl.

"Here is the salt," the foolish son said to his mother.

"But where is the flour?" the mother asked.

"In here," he replied, turning the bowl the right way up.

NINE

YOUTH
AND AGE

REASON GROWING DIM

Does your Reason now grow dim?
Do you now find it hard to think clearly?
Does logic seem like a hammer in your head,
Battering your soft brain into a pulp?

Perhaps age is weakening your mind.
Perhaps your Reason is fading with the years.
Or perhaps you have seen the limits of logic,
And recognized how little logic can discern.

Whether age or wisdom is the cause,
Welcome the confusion of your thoughts.
Out of chaos God created the world.
Out of confusion truth appears.

HANDSOME AND IMMORTAL

When I was young I thought I was immortal.
Death was for others, not for me.
I mocked old people for being old.
I would be young for ever.

When I was young I thought I was handsome.
Ugliness was for others, not for me.
I mocked plain people for being plain.
I would be young for ever.

Now I am old and ugly.
I hear the echoes of my former jibes.
Yet what good would youth now do me?
What would I do with beauty?

THE MARCH OF YEARS

Now you are strong and healthy, full of vigor.
But do not boast of your physical prowess.
At any moment illness may strike;
And the march of time will defeat your body.

Enjoy your strength and health while they last.
But do not make them your only pleasure.
Even now be happy with quietness;
Then the march of years cannot defeat your soul.

THE NIGHT OF CONCEPTION

My life began on the bed where I was conceived.
I think of the pleasure my parents enjoyed
    that night.
Did they conceive me in their minds that
    joyous time,
Or was it just a congress of their flesh?
Has my life been worthy of their highest hopes,
Or have I been a failure in their eyes?
Though I myself am parent of many children,
I still yearn for the approval of my parents.
In my mind they are my constant audience,
And I the performer for their inspection.
Let me break free from their quizzical gaze,
And remember the judge that truly counts – God.

LIFTING THE BURDEN

Throughout my life I have never confessed my sins.
I have never apologized to people I hurt.
I have never sought to make amends.
I have assumed time would blot out my wrongs.

But now I am old and close to death.
The sins of my past lie heavy on my soul.
I can still recall the wrongs I have done.
Time has not blotted them out.

To confess now would cost me nothing.
Those whom I hurt are old or dead.
There is nothing I could do to make amends.
How can this burden be lifted?

The Lord alone can set me free.
In him alone can I put my trust.

PASSING TIME

To a child a few weeks seem long.
To a youth a few months seem long.
To an adult a few years seem long.
To an old person decades seem short.

The old person is closest to God.
To God decades are seconds, centuries minutes.
To God eternity is every moment.
Be patient with yourself; think like God.

STRIVING FOR SUCCESS

When I was striving for success,
To make my mark upon the world,
I committed many sins,
I exploited many people
In order to achieve my purposes.
When my conscience pricked, I said:
"All will be justified when my task is done."

Now that I have finished striving,
And no longer want to make more marks,
I want only to be pure,
And to live in harmony with the world.
I see no difference between action and purpose;
The action is the purpose, the purpose the action.
"All must be justified here and now."

AN OLD NEIGHBOR

My neighbor is an old man.
He is so frail he can do no work.
His wife and children all have died.
So daily I must bring him food
And weekly I must clean his house.
Sometimes he smiles and thanks me,
More often he sits and scowls.
But gratitude is not my reward.
I simply hope when I am like him,
Someone will feed me and clean my house.
Daily I ask God to take him,
But I will miss him when he's gone.

AM I A BURDEN?

Am I a burden, now I am old?
My deaf ears force you to shout.
My wobbly legs force you to clean for me.
My bent fingers force you to sew for me.
My twisted back forces you to dress me.
My fading eyes force you to lead me.
My toothless mouth forces you to make soup
    for me.
Will you be pleased when I die?

Yet you tell me you love me.
You enjoy listening to my stories.
You ask me my advice.
You make me feel important.
I still need to be needed –
And you express your mind.
If you are deceiving me,
God bless you for your deception.

BUSY BEES

Bees get busy in summer,
Flying from flower to flower,
Getting honey or food for winter.

Let the young be busy in youth,
Skipping from pleasure to pleasure,
Getting memories as food for age.

GOOD HEALTH

The young take health for granted.
They are strong, robust, vigorous,
Yet do not notice these wonderful gifts
Because they have always possessed them.

The old yearn for health to return.
They are weak, frail, tired,
So they envy the gifts of youth,
Yet know they are gone for ever.

Could not the old become young and the
    young old?
Let the young be frail, and pray for strength;
And let their prayers be answered as years pass.
No: frailty prepares us for heaven.

TEN

LIFE
AND DEATH

GOD'S FLOCK

When you go out on the hills to tend your flock,
You ask yourself daily, "Have any gone astray?"
So you count your sheep one by one;
And if any are missing, you start to search.

We are God's flock, and the hills are God's world.
God asks daily: "Have any gone astray?"
So God counts his sheep one by one;
And if any are missing, God starts to search.

When winter comes, you round up your sheep,
And you and your dogs lead them to shelter.
It's too late to search.
The wandering sheep die on the hills.

When death comes, God rounds up his sheep,
And God and the angels lead them to heaven.
It's then too late to search.
The wandering sheep die in hell.

We know when winter is coming,
But death may come at any time.
So do not wander from God's flock,
Lest you're away when the searching stops.

THE LITTLE GREY CROW

The little grey crow with a bald head,
And the lark whose bed is the sky,
Must go where the fame of people must go,
And where people themselves must go.

All who have come, have gone,
All who now come, must go,
All who will come, shall go
To where the grace of God flows for ever.

ONLY A BREATH AWAY

You may be a scholar, able to speak Greek
    and Hebrew;
But in death only the language of God matters.

You may be a craftsman, able to fashion
    fine furniture;
But in death only God's spiritual handiwork
    survives.

You may be a musician, able to play the harp
    and lyre;
But in death only the Spirit's music persists.

You may be a priest, able to recite long prayers;
But in death only prayers of the heart are heard.

Death is only a breath away.
So listen for God's word,
Be transformed by God's hand,
Move to God's rhythm,
And pray to God with all your heart.

TRUE HEROES

How strange it is that military commanders
Who have killed countless thousands in battle,
And whose soldiers have pillaged numerous
    homes,
Are fêted as great heroes,
Their names recorded in history.

Yet humble men and women of the soil
Who labor day by day in the fields
Producing food to sustain bodily life
Are regarded as insignificant,
Their names forgotten when they die.

Does this mean we prefer death to life?

WHO ARE WAITING

Who are waiting for me to die?
Who are watching my failing body?

There is the devil
Wanting to entice my soul to hell.

There are my children
Wanting to inherit my land and gold.

There is the worm
Wanting to eat my rotting flesh.

And there is God
Wanting me to come back home.

IMAGINE YOURSELF DYING

Imagine yourself to be dying.
Your breath is growing weaker,
Your limbs are growing colder,
Your eyes are growing darker,
The sound around you grows fainter.

Are you at peace?
Or are you anxious?

By truly imagining death,
You can know the state of your soul.

SUDDEN DEATH

Let me not die suddenly.
I want to be warned of my impending death.
I need time to order my material affairs,
And time to confess my sins and repent.

But surely I could always keep my affairs in order.
Surely I could confess my sins as soon as I commit
    them.
Then I would be ready whenever God wanted me.
I would be happy to die suddenly.

THE PLAGUE STRIKES

When an epidemic strikes, people turn to prayer,
Asking God to save them from the vile plague.
Then they are affronted if prayer goes unanswered:
"This is not the action of a loving God."

Why did they not pray when all was well?
They thought they did not need God's grace.
True prayer enables us to face the plague:
"Even this is the action of a loving God."

A BRANCH BREAKING

The doctor tells me I am dying.
I can feel the pain that will kill me.
I am like a branch breaking in the wind,
A rock pulled by waves from the cliff.

Yet strangely I feel no fear.
I am ready to be broken and smashed.
I will live more fully now I am dying.
And the pain in my body shall remind me of both.

LOSING CONTROL

By strength of will we may stave off sleep.
One night, even two, we may keep ourselves
    awake.
But when our body rests, sleep overwhelms us,
In sleep we lose control of our minds.
The events in dreams are beyond all reason.

Sleep is like death, death like sleep.
We may delay the moment of death;
But death will overtake us – we cannot prevent it.
In death we lose control of our destiny.
The events beyond death are in the mercy of God.

STRETCHING OUT

I stretch myself out on this bed,
As in the coffin I shall be stretched.
I ask God to give me sweet dreams,
As in death I shall ask to enter heaven.
I look forward to rising again in the morning,
As after death I look forward to rising with Christ.

Let me rest as peacefully as I shall rest in my coffin;
May my dreams carry me to heavenly joy;
May I rise with fresh vigor to walk with Christ.

LYING DOWN WITH GOD

I lie down with God; may God lie down with me.
I sleep with God; may God be present in my
    dreams.
I trust in God; may God protect me from all danger.

I rise up with God; may God rise up with me.
I walk with God; may God always be at my side.
I rely on God; may God strengthen me in my labor.

I eat with God; may God be in my bread.
I drink with God; may God be in my wine.
I live with God; may God live within me.

SPARING THE FIRE

Each night I spare the fire,
My last act before retiring.
I bury two fresh lumps of peat
Deep within the embers.
Then tomorrow when I wake
I can poke the fire to life.

At death may God spare me.
When they bury my body
Deep within the boggy peat,
May my soul continue to glow.
So when the last trumpet sounds
I can rise with Christ to life.

REMEMBER YOUR END

Body, remember your end.
You feed yourself richly now
On red meat and sweet fruit.
But soon you shall be meat and fruit
To the worms of the earth.
You clothe yourself warmly now
In fine tunics and colorful cloaks.
But soon the damp red clay
Shall be your tunic and cloak.

Body, remember your end.
Then you will know
That you are only a temple,
A temporary abode,
For the immortal soul.

BEGINNING AND END

The first of a ship – wood planking,
The first of a kiln – stone heaping,
The first of a feast – good greeting,
The first of good health – sound sleeping.

The end of a ship – deep drowning,
The end of a kiln – red burning,
The end of a feast – black frowning,
The end of good health – sound sleeping.

THE PRIEST AND THE SOUL

Priest   Why are you sitting on this rock, weeping and wailing? How long have you been here?

Soul   I've been here 20 years. When I had an earthly body, I was a wretched sinner. When my body died, I didn't go to either heaven or hell, but stayed here.

Priest   Why does God not punish you for your sins?

Soul   This is my punishment. I must wait here until someone comes along, to whom I can confess my sins, and be absolved.

Priest   I am a priest. Confess your sins to me.

Soul   I have waited here so long that I have forgotten my sins; so I cannot confess them. I fear I must stay here for ever. That is why I am weeping and wailing.

Priest   If you cannot confess your sins, then at least you can make amends for them.

Soul   How can a soul without a body do anything on this earth?

Priest   If you had a body, you would only be able to talk to people. But without a body, you can actually enter them.

Soul   How can I help people by entering them?

Priest   People do not believe the truth about God and Jesus, about sin and virtue, about heaven and hell, just because priests like me teach them. They believe because they feel these things inside themselves. You can give people faith by teaching them from within.

Soul   Will I be the first soul to act in this way?

Priest   Not at all. There are countless souls like you. Those of us with bodies can feel them, but not see them. That is why certain places have a powerful effect on us – there are many souls there.

Soul   Very well, I will do as you say. And may God take me soon to heaven.

THE THREE PRIESTS

There were three priests living in a small town. One wanted to preserve the old simple Celtic styles of religion: "I abide by the traditions of Patrick and Brigit, the founders of our church," he said. The second wanted to adopt the new sophisticated styles and doctrines of the Roman church: "I want to be part of the universal church under the pope in Rome – and that is what Patrick and Brigit wanted," he said. The third said, "Let people worship and believe as they think best; if religion is just going to cause divisions, I want none of it."

These three priests remained friends, and often met for dinner; but their meetings always ended in argument. Sometimes they argued about how certain rituals should be performed. Sometimes they argued about heaven, and who would get there. "I believe that only those who remain loyal to the old Celtic traditions will get to heaven," the first said. "I believe that only those who accept the authority of the pope in Rome will be saved," the second said. "Let each person try to lead a good and honest life," the third said, "and then God will be the judge."

Some years later the three priests died, and arrived at the gate of heaven. Peter took the hand of the first priest. "Welcome, friend," Peter said, "you go and sit over there among the others who preserved the Celtic traditions." Then Peter took the hand of the second priest. "Welcome, friend," Peter said, "you go and sit over there among the others who have obeyed the pope in Rome." Finally Peter took the hand of the third priest. "Welcome, friend," he said, "you are free to wander wherever you want."

So the third priest wandered freely amongst all the different groups in heaven. And amongst the other people he saw wandering amongst the different groups were Patrick and Brigit – and Jesus Christ himself.

BIBLIOGRAPHY

If you wish to dig more deeply into the tradition of Celtic parables, these books are excellent, and can still be found in some libraries.

Flower, R. E. W. *Poems and Translations.*
    Constable & Co. Ltd., 1931.

Graves, A. P. *A Celtic Psaltery.* SPCK, 1917.

Gregory, Lady. *Poets and Dreamers.* Colin Smythe,
    1974. First published by John Murray, Hodges,
    Figgis & Co. Ltd., and Scribners in 1903.

Hull, E. *The Poem-Book of the Gael.*
    Chatto & Windus, 1912.

Hyde, D. *The Religious Songs of Connacht.*
    Irish University Press, 1972. First published by
    M. H. Gill & Son Ltd. and T. Fisher Unwin, 1906.

Meyer, K. *Ancient Irish Poetry.* Constable, 1994.
    A facsimile reprint of *Selections from Ancient Irish
    Poetry*, 2nd edition, Constable & Co., 1913.

Sharp, E. *Lyra Celtica.* Patrick Geddes & Colleagues,
    1896.

Synge, J. M. *The Aran Islands*. Penguin, 1992.
First published by Maunsel & Co., 1907.

Wilde, Lady. *Ancient Legends, Mystic Charms, and Superstitions of Ireland*. Ward & Downey, 1887.

Yeats, W. B. *The Celtic Twilight*. Prism Press, 1990.
First published by Lawrence and Bullen, 1893.